Against the Grain

AGAINST THE GRAIN

Insights from an Economic Contrarian

PAUL ORMEROD

Institute of
Economic Affairs

First published in Great Britain in 2018 by
The Institute of Economic Affairs
2 Lord North Street
Westminster
London SW1P 3LB
in association with London Publishing Partnership Ltd
www.londonpublishingpartnership.co.uk

The mission of the Institute of Economic Affairs is to improve understanding of the fundamental institutions of a free society by analysing and expounding the role of markets in solving economic and social problems.

A CIP catalogue record for this book is available from the British Library.

ISBN 978-0-255-36755-4

Many IEA publications are translated into languages other
than English or are reprinted. Permission to translate or to reprint
should be sought from the Director General at the address above.

Typeset in Kepler by T&T Productions Ltd
www.tandtproductions.com

Printed and bound in Great Britain by Page Bros

CONTENTS

THE AUTHOR

Paul Ormerod is an economist, author and entrepreneur. He is currently a Visiting Professor at University College London (UCL), where he supervises graduate students in machine learning.

Paul read economics at Cambridge and took an MPhil in economics at Oxford. He was elected a Fellow of the British Academy of Social Sciences in 2006, and in 2009 was awarded a DSc *honoris causa* by the University of Durham for the distinction of his contribution to economics. In addition to economic journals, he has published in journals such as *Nature, Proceedings of the National Academy of Sciences, Proceedings of the Royal Society of London* B and *Evolution and Human Behavior.* Paul has published four best-selling books on economics: *Death of Economics, Butterfly Economics, Why Most Things Fail* and *Positive Linking.* He has also written for the IEA on many occasions. He was a founder of the Henley Centre for Forecasting Ltd., which the management sold to Martin Sorrell's WPP Group in the 1990s.

FOREWORD

Since 2012 Paul Ormerod has ensured that hundreds of thousands of *City A.M.* readers are offered a short, sharp espresso shot of morning stimulation on their commute into London.

The original name of Paul's column was *Against the Grain*. It was a fitting title for a few hundred words that each week has offered an original, contrarian and thought-provoking take on the relationship between economic theory, individuals and policy.

I inherited Paul as a columnist from my predecessors in the editor's chair, and though I've made a few changes to the newspaper in the two and a half years since I started, I'm delighted that Paul's column has remained a fixture. Doubtless he'd have something to say about the economics of inherited wealth (or privilege, in this instance) but I'm immensely grateful that he continues to share his insight and analysis with our readers, even as the pages change around him.

As a newspaper, our main patches of interest are business, finance, economics and politics – and in Paul we have a writer who can pull them all together in his own inimitable style. At a time when economic statistics and forecasts can be deployed in support of whatever argument our politicians or Westminster wonks wish to advance, Paul rises above the fray and guides the reader towards a different point of view and a fresh perspective.

A respected academic himself, he has never held back from lambasting the profession for its groupthink or its leftward drift. In doing so he embodies the values of *City A.M.*, as we strive to question the consensus and hold true to the liberal, free-market values upon which the newspaper was built.

I hope that Paul will stay with us on this journey for years to come, and while we look forward to the columns not yet written, we can now dip into his wisdom at leisure thanks to this timely and important effort to collate his contributions.

The inquisitive reader will be able to find fresh thinking on some of the biggest issues of the day: automation, productivity, growth, the future of capitalism and the rise of artificial intelligence. For intelligence of the old-fashioned variety, I commend this book to you – and thank Paul for the immense contribution he has made to *City A.M.* over the years.

CHRISTIAN MAY
Editor-in Chief, City A.M.
January 2018

1 INTRODUCTION

In the summer of 2012, I was invited to write a weekly opinion column for *City A.M.* newspaper. It is a free, business-focused newspaper, launched in 2005, and is distributed at more than 250 commuter hubs across London and the Home Counties, as well as 1,600 offices throughout the City, Canary Wharf and other areas of high business concentration. The paper has a strong online presence at www.cityam.com.

The general views of the newspaper are broadly supportive of the free-market economy, of capitalism and private enterprise.

It is therefore very appropriate that this selection of my columns is being supported and published by the Institute of Economic Affairs.[1] As Allister Heath, editor of *City A.M.* from 2008 to 2014 and now editor of the *Sunday Telegraph*, wrote: 'the IEA is the home of good economic analysis applied to public policy.'

---

1 I would like to express my appreciation to *City A.M.* for carrying my pieces over the past few years, and to the Institute of Economic Affairs for republishing them. It is a pleasure to be associated with both these organisations. A special debt of gratitude is due to Len Shackleton of the University of Buckingham and the IEA.

As a description of what I aim to do in my columns, Allister Heath's statement could hardly be bettered. In the confines of 500 words each week, I try to shed light on a contemporary issue in political economy.

I use the phrase 'political economy' rather than 'economics' deliberately. The great founding figures of the discipline in the late eighteenth and early nineteenth centuries, such as Adam Smith and David Ricardo, regarded themselves as addressing broad questions of public import, rather than being confined to mere technical analysis.

In the mid-twentieth century, it was Friedrich Hayek, Nobel Laureate and a great inspirational figure for the IEA, who encapsulated this view:

> The physicist who is only a physicist can still be a first class physicist and a most valuable member of society. But nobody can be a great economist who is only an economist—and I am even tempted to add that the economist who is only an economist is likely to become a nuisance if not a positive danger.

The point simply cannot be made too frequently that we have seen several major natural experiments, which contrast the performances of economies based upon market-oriented principles with those based upon the planned economy principles of socialism. These contrasts include the United States and the Soviet Union, East and West Germany, North and South Korea, India and China under different forms of socialism and India and China under different forms of capitalism. Venezuela is but the latest example of a failing socialist experiment. Countries which were very poor in the mid-twentieth century and which have adopted the principles of market-oriented economics, however, have since flourished.

The key task of political economy is to provide a scientific understanding of how capitalism – by far the most successful social and economic system which humans have invented – actually works.

This book

Each of the sections of this book has its own fairly short introduction. This is meant to set the scene for how the overall topic of the section fits into economics. These discussions are not meant in any way to supplant economics textbooks or offer a comprehensive survey of the scientific literature on the topic. They are intended to provide a bit more information on each topic than is possible in this general introduction.

There is also a short note before each article, describing how it fits in and explaining the particular context in which it was written.

There is intended to be a structure to the sequence in which the sections, into which the articles are grouped, appear. Inevitably, there is quite often some overlap, and a piece will have points which are relevant to headings other than the one under which it appears. This reflects the fact that many aspects of the modern world are complex, and economists need to call on a range of different concepts in their analyses.

The collection starts with the area where economics is at its very strongest, and where knowledge of economics greatly assists the understanding of what might otherwise be puzzling phenomena. This is of course the area of market structures and incentives, which are fundamental to the success of the market-oriented economies of capitalism.

A wide range of issues can be analysed under this broad heading, and the scope of the pieces reflects this fact. This is also by some considerable margin the longest section of the book, reflecting the importance of markets and incentives in economics.

The other sections contain articles on themes where either economics is still very much grappling with how to tackle the problems, or where fresh approaches might be needed.

One section, in acknowledgment of the seminal work of Hayek, is on the limits to knowledge and the inherent uncertainty which surrounds many human decisions. Closely related to this, though discussed in a separate section, is the theme of innovation.

Following on from this, there is a group of pieces set out under the heading of 'networks'.

The last section is the area where I am most critical of existing economics, and the area which most grabs the attention of the media: macroeconomics.

This is not the place to discuss at length my views on the developments in economics over the past fifty years or so. Interested readers can see them in a chapter in Johnson et al. (2017). But a short overview may be useful both in understanding the rationale of grouping the pieces into their different sections, and giving a broad perspective on their general themes.

Microeconomics and macroeconomics

Like any academic discipline, economics is divided up into various different areas of study. The most important of these is a very simple one. An academic paper or lecture is either about 'micro' economics or 'macro' economics.

The American humourist P. J. O'Rourke rather neatly captured what has traditionally been the distinction between the two in his book *Eat the Rich*[2] (O'Rourke 1998):

> One thing that economists do know is that the study of economics is divided into two fields, 'microeconomics' and 'macroeconomics'. Micro is the study of individual behaviour, and macro is the study of how economies behave as a whole. That is, microeconomics concerns things that economists are specifically wrong about, while macroeconomics concerns things economists are wrong about generally.

Much of the focus in the media is on macroeconomics. For example, how much will the economy (GDP) grow next year? What will be the rate of inflation? Should austerity be abandoned? Economists frequently differ in their opinions on these topics.

---

2   The book is a very thoughtful and entertaining reflection on why some countries are rich and others poor.

But it is in fact the micro level which is the area in which most economics is done. Economics is essentially a theory about how individuals choose between alternatives in any given situation. And in this area, there is far more agreement than disagreement among professional economists, whether in universities, in commercial companies, in financial markets or in central banks.

My views on the two are easy to summarise. Over the past few decades, in my opinion, microeconomics has made a lot of progress. The same cannot be said of macroeconomics, which in some important respects has gone backwards.

Just one slightly technical point is appropriate here. In the paragraphs immediately above, reference is made to individual behaviour. The theory is more general than just individual humans.

Economists themselves often refer to 'agents' instead of 'individuals'. By this they mean, to use a rather cumbersome description, an individual decision-making unit. So, as well as being a person, it can be a firm, a government, a central bank, a regulatory body.

Economists certainly realise that a firm, say, is a complex entity. How decisions are made within a company is a complicated process. But for economists, the interest is in how the decisions of a firm affect other economic agents, its employees, its shareholders, its suppliers and so on. In other words, how the decisions impact on the environment external to the company.

So we make the simplifying assumption to treat a firm as a single decision-making unit, a single agent. How decisions are made within companies, we usually leave to other disciplines. In the same way, for example, we are not concerned with how an individual's brain works. Our interest is in the impact of decisions on other agents in an economic context. We are not trying to explain everything.

Economics has one very powerful scientific finding. Without an appreciation of this, it is not possible to provide more than a partial explanation, at best, of many economic and social phenomena.

It is probably the only general law in the whole of the social sciences: agents react to changes in incentives. In other words, if the set of incentives which an agent faces alters, the behaviour of the agent may change.

An everyday example of incentives is the behaviour of drivers when approaching a speed camera. Even the fiercest critic of economic theory is likely to slow down. The driver may have been exceeding the speed limit, but the probability of detection by the police, certainly on high-speed roads, is low. The probability rises sharply when a speed camera is present. The incentives faced by the driver have changed, and his or her behaviour changes as a result.

The above is an example of incentives involving money – the increased probability of being fined. But in a number of the pieces in the book, I give examples of how non-monetary incentives can also have a powerful influence on behaviour. It is a caricature of economics to believe that it is only concerned with prices.

Compared to fifty years ago, microeconomics offers a much richer and more realistic view of how this principle of incentives operates than does the popular view of 'rational economic person'.

In popular perception, this mythical individual ruthlessly gathers up a vast amount of information, and processes it in a computer-like way. From the whirrings of its brain, out pops the best possible decision to take – for that individual, and for that individual alone. There is a grain of truth in this rather grim representation of human nature in economics. But microeconomics has certainly softened the edges, and now offers a much more recognisably human portrait in its theoretical models.

I give just one example here, one which has been very influential in policy-making circles. Far from knowing everything there is to know about a given issue, the agent may only have access to limited amounts of information. Further, some agents may know more than others.

This concept was developed by George Akerlof and Joe Stiglitz. The press release for the award of the Nobel Prizes to them for their pioneering work stated:

> Borrowers know more than lenders about their repayment prospects. Managers and boards know more than shareholders about the firm's profitability, and prospective clients know more than insurance companies about their accident risk.

A great deal of the work of regulatory bodies involves trying to deal with this problem of 'information asymmetry'. Economists love to use grandiose phrases, but this simply means that, in a particular situation, different agents may have different amounts of information.

Following the original work of the Nobel Laureate Daniel Kahneman and his colleague Amos Tversky[3] in the 1970s, we have had an explosion of work in behavioural economics. Behavioural economics takes as its reference point how a rational agent would behave in any given context, and looks for empirical deviations from such behaviour. An excellent account of the development and achievements of behavioural economics is given in Thaler (2015).

Not all economists are as enamoured of behavioural economics as Thaler himself, who has made distinguished contributions to the field ever since he was inspired as a graduate student by the early work of Kahneman and Tversky. Many mainstream economists retain varying degrees of scepticism. For example, if a deviation from rationality is observed, is it just confined to that particular situation? Do we find it in other, similar situations, which from a scientific perspective would be much more impressive? Another question which is raised, and there are quite a few, is: Do the agents eventually learn to be rational? We might see a temporary move away from rational behaviour, but agents might correct this over time.

In a review of the book published in the IEA's academic journal *Economic Affairs*, I set out my own views on the strengths and weaknesses of behavioural economics (Ormerod 2016).

Alongside these developments, over the past four decades or so there have been important advances in the

---

3   Tversky died before their work was recognised by the Nobel Prize committee, and these prizes are never awarded posthumously.

statistical theory and practice of analysing large-scale databases containing information on individuals and the decisions which they have made. James Heckman and Daniel McFadden are probably the two most prominent names in this area, both of them being awarded the Nobel Prize. But the work is too heavily mathematical to warrant here more than this acknowledgement of its achievements. It plays an important role in many undergraduate and graduate courses in economics.

If microeconomics has moved forwards, the same cannot be said for macroeconomics. In terms of understanding the business cycle, the fluctuations in the total output of an economy, the central, self-imposed task in macroeconomics over the past forty years has been to develop models of the macro economy which are based upon the naive model of micro economic theory, effectively that of the caricature Rational Economic Person. This is ironic, given the massive progress which has been made in microeconomics over the same time period in making its models into more realistic descriptions of behaviour.

These macro models rapidly become mathematically very intricate, and it is easy to see the pure intellectual attraction for academics of working on them.

But policymakers often take a completely different view. Here, for example, is Jean-Claude Trichet, Governor of the European Central Bank during the economic crisis:

> When the crisis came, the serious limitations of existing economic and financial models immediately became apparent. Macro models failed to predict the crisis and

seemed incapable of explaining what was happening to the economy in a convincing manner. As a policy-maker during the crisis, I found the available models of limited help. In fact, I would go further: in the face of the crisis, we felt abandoned by conventional tools.[4]

My view that the mainstream macroeconomics of the business cycle has gone backwards is reflected in some of these *City A.M.* pieces. I am often critical of this aspect of the discipline because, for example, of its forecasting failures and for the fact that it does not make debt a central feature of its models.

Capitalist economies have two features which make them distinct from all previous and actually existing economic systems. One is the business cycle, the persistent fluctuations of the growth rates of GDP.

The second, which in many respects is *the* key feature of capitalism, is the fact that there has been steady but slow growth over time. Output and living standards expand. People are far better off now than they were in 1900. But a central element of the political economy of the current decade is that, in many economies, growth has not been rapid enough after the crash of the late 2000s.

Economics is not particularly well equipped to understand the process of growth. It is in essence a theory based upon market equilibrium, while growth necessarily involves change and disruption.

---

4   https://www.ecb.europa.eu/press/key/date/2010/html/sp101118.en.html (a 2010 speech in Frankfurt).

This disruption was a key theme in the work of a series of great economists, from Karl Marx in the mid-nineteenth century to Joseph Schumpeter in the mid-twentieth. It was Schumpeter who coined the phrase 'gales of creative destruction' to describe the disruptive transformations brought about by innovations.

The work of these economists – and others like Keynes and Hayek – was primarily descriptive. Modern economists, however, have become addicted to formal models. Robert Solow developed a mathematical model of growth in 1956, for which he subsequently received the Nobel Prize.

In Solow's model, the growth rate of an economy depends upon three things: the amount of labour used in the economy; the amount of capital used; and what Solow called 'technological progress', a synonym for innovation.

There have been flurries of further work building on this approach. The one thing of real value to have come out of it all is that empirical studies of growth suggest that it is innovation which does most of the work. And it is innovation which is the unexplained part of the model, the 'residual' as it is often described. So one theme which I cover in these *City A.M.* pieces is the importance of innovation.

Both micro- and macroeconomics face a new challenge, in the form of the internet economy. How do we actually behave in the internet economy, faced with a stupendous cornucopia of choice? It is not possible to process all the available information. For example, in the middle of typing these words, I googled the phrase 'mobile phones'. I received 'about 155,000,000 results'. 155 million sites!

We need not throw out the rational choice model, but we need to modify it in many contexts to take into account that we often need to make quite drastic short cuts. A central problem in making choices has become not how to acquire information, but what information we should throw away and not even consider.

In practice, a good way of doing this is to take into account the decisions taken by a small number of other people whom we feel we can trust. Who these are will vary from context to context. I may decide, for example, that a particular website is reliable for restaurant reviews, or that my cousin knows about the merits of various airlines.

This introduces the importance of networks. Which people I pay attention to, the websites which I think are useful, are all part of the network of an individual in any given context. In terms of political discussion, Twitter has notoriously become an 'echo chamber'. People with similar views tweet and retweet each other, and rarely engage with others of different opinions.

Economists are at last starting to appreciate the potential importance of networks. For example, central banks are showing great interest in the networks which connect banks through the pattern of assets and liabilities, and the possibility that a cascade of failure might percolate across the network. An issue in 2014 of the leading American Economic Association journal, the *Journal of Economic Perspectives*, carried a symposium of papers on the topic of networks.

Sources

The pieces in this book often refer to a policy-oriented report or to an academic article. A Google search should enable these to be accessed readily, and a list of references is also provided at the end of each section.

These primary sources vary widely in their accessibility to the general reader. It is emphatically not necessary to use mathematics to discuss interesting and challenging ideas in political economy. But mathematics does have its uses, especially in clarifying the circumstances in which we would expect to see a particular outcome.

Alfred Marshall, mentioned several times in the main text, founded the department of economics at the University of Cambridge in 1903. Marshall himself was originally a mathematician, indeed he was placed second across the whole university in his final examinations. He made extensive use of maths in advancing economics. Yet one of his key injunctions was that if he could not translate these results into English, he would then 'burn the maths'.

I do try to make abstruse mathematical and statistical papers accessible by translating them into English, though the original academic articles of this genre will remain difficult for the general reader.

Finally, for clarification, the pieces are in the form of the original drafts which I submitted to the newspaper. I have not amended them in any way in the light of subsequent events, although in a few of them a brief update on the topic being discussed is provided.

I have had three excellent editors at *City A.M.* over the years, Phillip Salter, Tom Welsh and now Rachel Cunliffe. The pieces published by *City A.M.* contain their edits. But the printed articles and those available online are not always exactly the same, reflecting the slightly different space constraints of the two. The main points in the original pieces remain unchanged, however, and Jamie Whyte, Research Director at the IEA, solved the question of which version to publish here by saying decisively: 'stick with the originals!'

References

Hayek, F. (1967) *Studies in Philosophy, Politics and Economics*, chapter 8. Chicago University Press.

Johnson, J., Ormerod, P., Rosewell, B., Nowak, A. and Zhang, Y.-C. 2017 *Non-Equilibrium Social Science*. Springer. (Available at https://link.springer.com/book/10.1007%2F978-3-319 -42424-8 under the Creative Commons License.)

Ormerod, P. (2016) Picking up the gauntlet: Richard Thaler's defence of behavioural economics. *Economic Affairs* 36(1): 91–101.

O'Rourke, P. J. (1998) *Eat the Rich: A Treatise on Economics*, p. 108. New York: Atlantic Monthly Press.

Thaler, R. H. (2015) *Misbehaving: The Making of Behavioral Economics*. New York: W. W. Norton.

2 MARKET STRUCTURES AND INCENTIVES

It is easy to caricature economics. The basic textbook model describes a single market with a demand curve and a supply curve. The demand curve describes how the amount purchased falls as the price of the product increases, and the supply curve shows how supply rises with price. Both consumers and producers react rationally to price changes, which is the only factor which influences their behaviour. Price moves to bring demand and supply into balance with each other, so that the market is in equilibrium.

So, in this model we have Rational Economic Person, who is solely motivated by monetary factors – how cheaply you can buy the product and how expensively you can sell it. And we have the notion of equilibrium, that the economy is capable of ensuring that demand is equal to supply.

Particularly since the financial crisis, the concepts of rational economic behaviour and equilibrium have been widely ridiculed, especially by the Left. Like any caricature, it contains an element of truth. This is certainly the case with modern academic macroeconomics, as we shall see in the final chapter of this book.

But economics itself is far more subtle than the simple textbooks make it appear. Markets and monetary incentives are indeed fundamental tools in the kit which is used by economists.

But there are many sophisticated add-ons, as it were, which are needed to analyse the real world. Even apparently simple situations can require considerable reflection, and the application of a range of concepts, in order to understand them.

An excellent illustration of this is provided by an article which was published over seventy years ago.

R. A. Radford was a student at Cambridge when World War II broke out in 1939. He joined the army, and was captured in North Africa in 1942, spending the rest of the war in a prisoner-of-war camp in Germany.[1] He shared this experience with many young men of a similar age.

Radford was one of the few who was studying economics. But what makes him really interesting is that, shortly after the war, he published an academic paper on the economic organisation of his prisoner-of-war camp.

The article is readily available.[2] It is also very accessible, being wholly and completely in English. There is not a single mathematical symbol in the entire piece. It is hard to find a better example of how markets emerge, how they operate, and how they improve human lives.

---

1 The experience does not seem to have done him lasting harm. He went on to have a successful career at the International Monetary Fund, and lived to the age of 87.

2 http://icm.clsbe.lisboa.ucp.pt/docentes/url/jcn/ie2/0POWCamp.pdf

In general, the Germans treated Allied prisoners of war tolerably well. The prisoners were provided with basic rations, augmented with occasional Red Cross parcels. They were not required to work. So no goods were produced, and the inmates could not obtain wages in a labour market.

The economic structure corresponded pretty closely to what economists describe as being a pure exchange economy – a really simplified, stripped down version of a modern economy. As Radford writes, 'despite a roughly equal distribution of resources [among the prisoners], a market came into spontaneous operation, and prices were fixed by the operation of supply and demand'.

In many ways, it is a textbook example of how markets work. But despite the very simple social structure in which the markets operated, many nuances arose. Even here, supply and demand were not the only factors to take into account. And Radford, as a good economist, was aware of them.

For example, false information, such as rumours of an imminent Allied victory, could distort the workings of the market and lead to speculative bubbles in prices. Further, the prisoners tended to keep to their own huts, and middle men, as they called them, appeared. These carried out arbitrage, looking for opportunities to buy cheap in one hut and sell dear in another.

The best example of this was the case of one particular man who was able to capitalise his knowledge of Urdu by buying tinned meat from the essentially non-English speaking Sikh hut and selling butter and jam in return. The quasi-monopoly profits he earned, however, attracted other entrants into this market, and they were largely competed away.

Markets and incentives are fundamental features of the world. Understanding how they work in any particular context is the real challenge of economics.

As mentioned in the Introduction, specific reports and articles which are a feature of a particular piece are collected in the references at the end of each chapter, and cited in the summary.

Meat and potato pies and the Nobel Prize in economics

Even apparently simple situations require subtle economic reasoning in order to understand them. This piece uses economic theory to explain key aspects of behaviour when the pies ran out at half time in the humble setting of a Football League Division Two (the lowest division) match played during the Christmas holidays (Ostrom 2009; Stiglitz 2001).

Tragedy struck at a mid-week game played during the holiday season in Football League Division Two. The pies ran out in the home supporters' bar. The incident may seem trivial to those not involved. Yet it illustrates some important themes in economics, which have even gained their inventors the Nobel Prize.

It turns out that the number of away fans was higher than expected. No surprise here. Even distinguished teams of economists regularly make errors in their predictions. Because of this forecasting failure, the away pies ran out first. The away fans are charged 50p more for a pie, so the powers that be rapidly diverted pies away from the home team bar. Not on account of politeness towards the visitors. There was simply more profit to be made. Incentives matter. This is why, for example, the Coalition is keen to reward work rather than benefits.

But how can this price differential exist? The pies sold to both home and away fans are identical in terms of their quality. Here is where Joe Stiglitz enters the scene. Stiglitz is famous now for his polemics on macroeconomic policy. But he received his Prize for inventing the concept of asymmetric information and showing its consequences for economic theory.

The home supporters have much more information about the price of pies. They buy them every week. But the away fans lack this detailed knowledge. They have a rough idea of the general price of a pie, but lack specific local information and so are happy to pay what is, unbeknown to them, the 50p premium.

Mobile phone companies make great use of this concept. Both phone rentals and phone calls are simple enough products, which should be easy to compare across suppliers. But many of the companies appear to make the tariffs as confusing as possible. In so doing, they create asymmetric information. The firms know what is going on. The customers find it hard to work out and compare offers.

Why did trade not spring up in the pies, arbitraging away some of the price differential? Enterprising home fans could have bought a dozen each and offered them to the away fans at only 25p more, say, creating profit for themselves and benefiting the visitors. A market opportunity seems to have gone missing.

An important reason is the lack of an institutional framework which would create trust among the potential buyers in what might have been offered to them. The away supporters would not unreasonably be suspicious of what was going on if rival fans tried to sell them pies at lower prices. The importance of trust for markets to function properly was a key theme of Nobel Laureate Elinor Ostrom, who sadly died last year. And trust, or rather the lack of it, is a red hot topic in financial circles right now.

9 January 2013

Incentives, scarce resources and the refugee crisis

The waves of refugees from the various crises in North Africa and the Middle East had become a major political topic during the late summer of 2015. The piece shows that economics can show how to obtain better outcomes, even in emotionally fraught situations.

Emotions are running high over the refugee crisis. The heartbreaking images have aroused waves of compassion across Europe. As ever, economics lurks in the background. Underlying realities are not altered by the feelings stirred up by stories of human tragedy.

We can contrast the general composition of the refugees fleeing Syria and those already encamped at Calais. The Syrians are mainly family groups, whereas in Calais young men predominate. Incentives help explain their choices of destination. As they trail across Eastern Europe, the Syrians chant 'Germany!' At Calais everyone wants to get into the UK. The political situation is highly fluid, but Germany has had a policy of open borders for such refugees. Other European countries are less easy to get into.

Those in Calais speak fluent English and have high skill levels. They would make a much more positive contribution to this country than, say, relatives imported from the poorest parts of Pakistan and Bangladesh. Their families have invested large amounts of money in their journeys, made with the specific purpose of getting into the UK.

The lighter regulatory burden imposed on the British labour market than in much of the rest of the EU is in many ways a great strength. But it does mean that it is much easier to work illegally here. In theory, employers can be prosecuted for employing illegal immigrants, but in practice this rarely happens. Skilled young people can thrive, which is why they want to come. Not to sponge off our benefits, but to work.

Incentives feature strongly in the highly emotive issue of the boat crossings. Since the EU took the decision to rescue the boats, the numbers have soared. The demand has increased after an important component of the price of the voyage, that of the chances of being drowned or turned back, has fallen sharply. The consequences of misguided liberalism have been to place more lives at risk.

Indeed, there is increasing evidence that the boat captains are now not even bothering to get on board themselves. They simply take their large fees and let the refugees steer as best they can. After all, why put your own time and effort into a task when the EU will, or at least purport to, do it for you? So the crossings have become even more dangerous.

The role of incentives is misunderstood and so, too, is the most fundamental feature of economics, namely the allocation of scarce resources. 'Saint' Bob Geldof may be able to accommodate refugees in his large underutilised homes, but for local authorities there is a real trade-off. Every refugee housed is a person already on the waiting list who has to stay on it. Not just that, they tend to be allocated to the poorer parts of the country where property is cheap. Simon Danczuk, the leading Labour moderate, points out that his Rochdale constituency has already been made to accept more asylum seekers than the whole of the South East of England.

Economics may often seem harsh, but keeping its principles in mind can avoid outcomes being even worse.

9 September 2015

The market for speeding points

In the textbooks, price is set in a market so that demand equals supply seems. But how does this price emerge? This was a key question posed by Vernon Smith, the founding father of experimental economics, in his Nobel Prize lecture in 2002 (Smith 2002).

The British public were fascinated by a dispute involving the then married couple Chris Huhne, a Liberal Democrat member of the UK coalition government Cabinet, and Vicky Pryce, a former Government Chief Economist. Allegations flew to and fro about whether Pryce had agreed to take a speeding point penalty incurred by Huhne. In early 2013, both were sentenced to short jail sentences, though Pryce, at least, has subsequently continued to enjoy a successful career in the public eye. The piece discusses how price is set in practice in many markets, using the market for speeding points – which does exist – as an example (Humphrey 1996).

What is it worth to take someone else's speeding points? The Huhne–Pryce case has brought this into sharp focus.

Setting aside the moral issues, the question raises interesting topics in economics.

It turns out that there is a market in these points. The *Daily Telegraph* discovered that prisoners are willing to take points. By the time they get out, the points will often have expired. For around £200, someone will take your three points. But mingling with a group of England supporters after the Wales debacle on Saturday,[3] their tongues loosened by alcohol, I discovered that one respectable woman claimed to have done it for £500.

How does this market work? How is the price actually decided? Like many questions in science, the ones which seem easy to ask are often the hardest to answer. Vernon Smith, economics Nobel prizewinner in 2002, noted as much in his acceptance speech when he stated, 'We do not understand why markets work as they do.'

The basic textbooks give a pat answer to how the price is set. It is a simple matter of supply and demand. Price is where supply equals demand. But the market for points is more complicated.

For example, there is a lack of transparency about other transactions. It is not prudent to enquire too extensively about what the going rate might be. Further, there is no institutional setting which regulates the conduct of the market to balance supply and demand at any point in time, so transactions can take place at what the textbook would regard as non-equilibrium prices.

---

3   The loss was in Rugby Union, which remains a largely middle- and upper-class game in England.

Leading economists wrestled with these problems at the turn of the nineteenth century, when economic theory was first formalised. Alfred Marshall founded the economics department at Cambridge around 1900. His contemporary, Edgeworth, believed that there was inherent uncertainty about the outcome of the interplay between supply and demand.

In any given situation, there would be a range of potential outcomes for price. He developed a useful tool, the Edgeworth box, for thinking about it. Marshall simply assumed the problem away, and Marshallian diagrams of supply and demand, each with a uniquely determined price, have dominated economics textbooks ever since.

Interest in these problems has revived in the twenty first century. In many financial markets, for example, prices are set by a formal set of rules known as a continuous double auction. It seems to be the case, for reasons we do not yet fully understand, that this process itself generates some of the key features of changes in financial asset prices such as 'fat tails' – the fact that very large changes, while rare, are much more frequent than financial regulators believed before the crash.

Increasingly, the world is full of complex products and services. Naive supply and demand analysis can only take us so far in understanding how their prices are set. Institutional structures, price-setting mechanisms, information flows, all these need adding to the mix. The market for speeding points illustrates key aspects of our modern world.

20 March 2013

Bacon sandwich with sugar, anyone?

The British government had just published a report by Public Health England (PHE) calling for a 20 per cent tax on sugary drinks and food. PHE claimed that if the tax reduced sugar intake in line with the recommendations, tens of thousands of deaths could be prevented in the next 25 years.

The piece gives examples which show that working out the reactions to this proposed change in incentives might not be quite as straightforward as PHE believe. Even in markets where price is the major determinant of behaviour, people can react in innovative and unexpected ways to changes in price (Adda and Cornaglia 2006).

Government ministers have bowed to pressure. They have published the report by Public Health England (PHE) which calls for a tax of up to 20 per cent on sugary drinks and foods. If the tax reduced sugar intake in line with the recommendations, it is claimed that more than 77,000 deaths could be prevented in the next 25 years. PHE must be gifted with unusual powers of clairvoyance to be able to see the future with such precise accuracy. Better get the staff transferred to the Treasury or the Bank pronto, so they can predict the next economic crisis!

Lurking in all such projections is the little word 'if'. It is this tiny word which is the downfall of so many grandiose plans of social engineering. The public may simply not believe the message, at least not in sufficient numbers to make much difference.

Hardly a week goes by without some pompous official proclaiming that something we have enjoyed since time immemorial is a mortal threat to our health.

The latest is the pronouncement from the World Health Organization that bacon sandwiches and sausages are as dangerous as smoking. Such statements are often contradicted at some point in the future. Car owners, for example, were actively encouraged to switch from petrol to diesel, but the latter is now regarded as the devil incarnate.

The fundamental difficulty is that ordinary people are much smarter and more creative in their reactions to changes in incentives than planners give them credit for. During the UN Climate Change conference in Copenhagen in 2009, the city council wanted to curb prostitution. They sent postcards to hotels and delegates urging them not to patronise the city's sex workers. The members of the Sex Workers Interest Group responded by offering free sex to anyone who could produce both their delegate card and one of the postcards sent by the Mayor. They faced the choice of a much reduced income if the Mayor's strategy was complied with, or a normal income reduced by the occasional free service.

Taxes on sugar are altogether less exotic. If the price goes up, less will be consumed. That is the opening chapter of many economic textbooks. But reality can be much more complex.

Different states in America have different levels of tax on cigarettes. Jerome Adda and Francesca Cornaglia of University College London took advantage of this to examine how smokers responded to different tax rates in a 2006 paper in the *American Economic Review*. The higher the rate of tax, the fewer cigarettes smoked. So far, so good. But higher rates led smokers to switch to brands with higher tar and nicotine yields. In addition, smokers increased their intensity of smoking by smoking right down to the butt. Such behaviour further increases tar and nicotine consumption, and leads to even more dangerous chemicals being inhaled.

Obesity is undoubtedly a serious problem. But the idea that a simple tax on sugar will solve the problem is a pure fantasy of the mindset of the central planner.

28 October 2015

Don't send bankers to jail.
Just don't give them knighthoods

Incentives need not involve price, or indeed monetary factors of any form. Price is indeed important, which is why it is the main feature of textbooks. But even by the time of Alfred Marshall, who founded the Cambridge faculty of economics in 1903 and who wrote the world best-seller textbook of his day, economists had known for a long time that price was not the only thing which mattered.

Bankers have behaved selfishly since time immemorial (Raw et al. 1971 is an entertaining and instructive example). The debate about how to prevent this continues to this day. Just before the piece was written, the Treasury Committee of the House of Commons had published a report on bankers and the crisis. This piece offers a slightly tongue-in-cheek suggestion of an incentive which really might alter their behaviour.

The behaviour of the banking sector in the run-up to the crash is still very much in the public eye. Readers of a certain age might recall Bernie Cornfeld and Investors Overseas Services (IOS). IOS was a pure financial scam on a massive scale. It encouraged the flight of capital from developing countries and tax evasion in the West.

Cornfeld lived an exceptionally flamboyant lifestyle, with mansions all over the world, throwing extravagant parties and living with a dozen girls at a time, movie stars, supermodels, princesses. The only penalty he suffered was eleven months in a Swiss jail.

It is not only bankers who might find such a trade-off attractive. So how do we manage to get the banks to behave responsibly? Cornfeld was a crook, but a very astute one. He remarked, 'If you want to make money, work directly with money. Don't horse around making light bulbs.'

People work in banks because they want to make money. Keynes wrote in the 1930s that if people in the financial sector were not driven by money, the work would be intolerably boring. He went on to say that the markets performed a useful social function. Many people in them exhibit serious pathological tendencies, and the pursuit of money diverts them from violence and crime.

The standard way of discouraging any activity like this is through changing the incentive structure. This is what lies behind the recent Parliamentary report recommending jail sentences for reckless bankers. Deterrence is important. But there are two parts to any deterrent. The severity of the penalty itself, and the probability of receiving it.

Andrew Tyrie's Parliamentary report says top bankers should not be able to use the defence that they did not know what was going on. But even if the law already permitted jail terms, how would the Co-op debacle be dealt with? It is allegedly due to the risky loans of the Britannia Building Society. When the Co-op took it over in 2009, these loans were certified as being acceptable by two sets of auditors as well as Lord Adair Turner's Financial Services Authority.

The motives of the report are perfectly understandable. The risk is that regulators with job security and gold-plated pensions will simply use the wisdom of hindsight to assign guilt. It is easy for a bureaucrat to say that if a loan ever goes bad, even years after it has been granted, someone must be to blame. Uncertainty about the future is an inherent part of the human condition.

Incentives do matter. But their real impact comes when they stimulate permanent changes in attitudes and values in the relevant social network. A statement that, for the next five years at least, no one from the City will be given a peerage, knighthood, or even invited to Buckingham Palace garden parties would work wonders. It would send the clearest possible message that the financial services sector needs to clean up its act.

26 June 2013

Would harsher punishments deter the likes of Twisleton-Wykeham-Fiennes?

There was outrage in the autumn of 2016 when the City of London airport was closed by Black Lives Matter protestors occupying the runways. It was felt particularly keenly when it emerged that they were all white and either upper middle class or genuine toffs. The piece discusses empirical evidence in economics on how incentives in the criminal justice system can deter crime – or reduce the supply, as we economists would say (Drago et al. 2009; Levitt and Dubner 2005).

Natalie Twisleton-Wykeham-Fiennes: don't you just love her? One of the Black Lives Matter campaigners, our Nat caused chaos by occupying the runway at City airport, on the grounds that climate change is racist. She and eight others, including a former member of the Oxford University Croquet Club, were sentenced by the courts last week. For many, their punishments were derisory: token fines and suspended prison sentences.

Would harsher treatment deter future protests like this and the one which disrupted Heathrow last month? Anecdotal evidence suggests it would. In the town where I grew up, nestling in the foothills of the Pennines, the police would often drive miscreant youths late at night to remote hamlets up on the moors and make them walk home. It helped if it was raining, which it usually was. The more recalcitrant were likely to discover that the damp made the steps of the local police station unusually slippery. Compared to today, crime was low.

But this is mere casual empiricism, and there is a vast academic literature on whether or not harsher punishments deter crime. As a broad approximation, criminologists themselves tend to be sceptical about the impact of punishment as a deterrent. A few years ago, I was at a seminar on the topic in which a criminology professor at Middlesex University asserted, without a trace of irony, that crime was caused by capitalism. In contrast, economists, who believe that agents respond to incentives, often claim that deterrence works.

Economists base their conclusions not just on theory, but on statistical analysis of detailed databases. Even so, the results might not be straightforward to interpret. For example, if prison sentences are increased and we see a fall in crime, is this because potential criminals are deterred, or because prolific criminals are in jail and can't commit crimes?

Francesco Drago and colleagues published an influential paper in the *Journal of Political Economy* in 2009. They exploited the natural experiment provided by the Collective Clemency Bill passed by the Italian Parliament in July 2006. This provided for an immediate reduction of three years in the sentences of existing inmates, and as a result 22,000 of them were released. But if they re-offended, they had to serve all the suspended time, plus whatever extra they were given. The study showed decisively that an additional month in expected sentence reduced the propensity to recommit a crime by 1.24 per cent. Steve Levitt, in his bestseller *Freakonomics*, described similar results obtained by smart analysis of American data.

Perhaps the way forward is to experiment with another fundamental concept in economics, that of externalities. Twisleton-Wykeham-Fiennes believes that flying, while convenient for the individual, imposes costs on others through its negative impact on the climate. Other people bear these costs, which are external to the benefits to the person flying. The airport protests inconvenienced many others. So the fines should be in proportion to the external costs created by the crime. The assets of the well-heeled protestors would vanish in a trice. Anyone for this natural experiment? Future Twisleton-Wykeham-Fienneses might prefer croquet instead.

21 September 2016

Why can't students learn? University is not worthwhile for most

Even when incentives operate broadly in line with expectations, it can take a long time for them to have their full effect. The next piece was published at the start of a new university year in the UK.

The Sunday Times had released a detailed survey about the earnings of graduates across both universities and courses.[4] *It was very clear well before this that the vaunted 'returns to education', which had led Tony Blair in the late 1990s to set a target for 50 per cent of each age cohort to attend university, did not operate for many graduates (Dolton and Vignoles 2000).*

Basic economics was at work. A big increase in supply had reduced the average price. But young people, despite the well-publicised evidence of this and other surveys, still want to go to university. They incur large debts in the process and

---

4 Material from *The Times* newspaper group is not generally available online, a subscription being required. Similar information on graduate salaries can be found at http://www.cityam.com/268464/average-graduate-salaries-university-and-subject-go-and and related links.

are not getting a return. Despite the incentive set which they face, they continue to make apparently irrational decisions. Student debt went on to become a major factor in the 2017 General Election in the UK.

An exciting time of the year for many young people, with some setting off to university for the first time, and others starting to polish their applications for next year. Good news if you have been accepted to read economics at Cambridge, say, or business studies at Oxford. A survey by the *Sunday Times* shows that the average salary, just six months after graduating, is over £40,000. If instead you are off to Worcester to do drama and dance or Liverpool Hope for psychology, you can expect around £13,000, just under half the value of average earnings across the workforce as a whole.

Figures like these raise the question of whether it is worthwhile studying many of the courses which are on offer. It is a question which is increasingly pressing. Last month, a report commissioned by the Chartered Institute of Personnel and Development (CIPD) claimed that no fewer than 58 per cent of the UK's graduates are in non-graduate jobs compared to only 10 per cent in Germany. The growth in graduates is outstripping the growth in high skilled jobs across the EU, but especially in Britain.

Successive government have made a fetish of higher education. The Conservatives elevated a whole raft of polytechnics to university status in 1992, followed by a second wave under New Labour in the 2000s. Tony Blair was insistent that his target be met of 50 per cent of each year group of young people going to university.

The mismatch between the supply of and demand for graduates is not something new. It was already well known when Blair invented his mantra of 'education, education, education'. Peter Dolton and Anna Vignoles, both then at Newcastle University, published a famous paper nearly twenty years ago on overeducation in the graduate labour market. Scientists measure the value of an academic paper by the number of citations it receives from other scholars. On this criterion, this one is a star.

They looked at a very large sample of graduates and their conclusion was stark. 'We find that 38% of graduates were overeducated for their first job and, even six years later 30% of the sample were overeducated.' So the current estimate of 58 per cent by the CIPD, twenty years later, startling though it may seem, may not be too far off the mark. To be fair, other studies do come up with lower numbers. But they all demonstrate the same point. Lots of graduates end up in jobs which do not require a degree.

This is bad news for economic theory, which predicts that even if overeducation is observed, it will only be a temporary phenomenon. Companies are assumed to adapt their production techniques to fully utilise the increased supply of skills.

Is it bad news for the students? A quantitative degree from a good university still commands a huge premium in terms of lifetime earnings. But estimates of the average amount extra that a graduate will earn conceal massive differences in outcomes. Increasingly, studying weak courses at weak institutions is simply not worthwhile.

28 September 2016

Can Nanny make you stop drinking?

When incentives change, the responses of people may very well differ at different points in time after the change. The point extends to the fashionable area of 'nudge' in behavioural economics (Allcott and Rogers 2014).

Nudge usually involves either changing non-monetary incentives, or altering the structure in which decisions are made so that people perceive the incentives in a different light.

The National Institute for Health and Care Excellence (NICE) announced that a pill designed to reduce alcohol consumption among problem drinkers would be made available across the NHS, but this attracted ridicule for its broad definition of problem drinking. The piece was written in response to the potential impact of 'nudges', which are increasingly used in a health context.

The National Institute for Health and Care Excellence (NICE) has been the butt of much ridicule over the past week. A pill designed to reduce alcohol consumption among problem drinkers will be made available across the NHS. But the concept of problem drinkers is so wide that it embraces people who enjoy a couple of modest glasses of wine a day. Indeed, the treatment is not really aimed at serious alcoholics who knock back litres of vodka with meths chasers.

There are now vast swathes of behaviour which Western governments attempt to modify. The government has its 'nudge' unit dedicated to precisely this end. Obesity, smoking, the amount of exercise people take, voting registration, recycling, energy consumption are some of the examples.

On the latter, it is not just the amount but the mix. Hectored for years that diesel fuel was morally superior to petrol, some unfortunates followed the advice and switched their cars to diesel. They now find themselves on the receiving end of a volte-face on the matter by the bureaucracy.

There is a literature in top-ranking economics journals on the impact of such interventions. In general, there is a short-term effect which gives the policymakers what they want, but gradually, the reactions become muted and people revert to their old patterns. There are exceptions, but most of these attempts to change behaviour fail.

An interesting paper in the latest *American Economic Review* by Hunt Allcott and Todd Rogers shows the enormous efforts which are needed to alter the decisions which people make in the long term. In the US, nearly 100 utilities hire a company called Opower to send home energy reports every month to millions of households. Households receive information on personal energy use, social comparisons and energy efficiency information.

The real interest in the Opower work is that some of the programmes were set up as controlled scientific experiments. Allcott and Rogers examine three of the longest-running ones, which started in the late 2000s. Highly sophisticated metering devices were installed. Households, from a very large sample, were selected at random to receive the information. And after two years, some of those getting the reports were randomly assigned to have them stopped. This way, both post-intervention persistence and the incremental effects of continued treatment can be measured.

Unsurprisingly, there is an immediate reduction in energy consumption after receipt of the first report, though this impact decays rapidly. In households discontinued after two years, the subsequent decline is much lower. The sheer frequency of the reports does seem to alter behaviour. But there are further reductions in energy consumption in households who continue to receive the information, suggesting that people take a very long time to completely change their habits.

In the UK, attitudes towards wearing seat belts and drink driving did eventually change, but it took a very long time. Short-term trendy campaigns to 'nudge' behaviour are just not going to work. Governments have to be in it for the long haul.

8 October 2014

Paying for performance can be bad. It's (almost) official

Incentive structures which are not thought through can often lead to undesirable outcomes. In July 2017, the BBC incurred serious wrath with the publication of the huge salaries paid to many of its staff. By pure coincidence, at the same time the 2016 Nobel prizewinner Bengt Holmström published his prize lecture in the American Economic Review on performance-based pay (Holmström 2017).

Holmström, despite being very much a mainstream economist, concluded that high-powered financial incentives are often dysfunctional and attempts to bring market principles into the firm usually misguided.

Following the disclosure of the salaries at the BBC, it has hardly seemed possible to open a newspaper or switch on the television without being bombarded by stories about pay.

By pure coincidence, an academic paper entitled 'Pay for performance and beyond' has just appeared. So what, you might ask? Except that it is one of the 2016 Nobel Prize lectures, by Bengt Holmström, a professor at MIT.

Holmström's work began in the 1970s on what is known in the jargon as the principal–agent problem. This is of great practical importance. For example, how should the owners of companies (the 'principals' in economic jargon) design contracts so that the interests of the directors (the 'agents') are aligned as closely as possible with the interests of the shareholders?

Many aspects of economics have a lot of influence on policymaking. But this is not yet one of them. We have only to think of the behaviour of many bankers in the run-up to the financial crisis. Stupendous bonuses were paid out the employees, and in examples such as Lehman Brothers the owners lost almost everything.

It is not just at the top levels that scandals occur. Towards the end of last year, Wells Fargo had to pay $185 million in penalties. Holmström cites this prominently in his lecture. The performance of branch managers was monitored daily. They discovered that one way of doing well was to open shell accounts for existing customers. These were accounts which the customers themselves did not know about, but they counted towards bonuses.

A culture of pressure to perform against measured criteria can lead to problems even when the organisations involved are not strongly driven by money. The education system in the UK has many examples. But the one given by Holmström is even more dramatic. The No Child Left Behind Act of 2001 in the US was very well intentioned. But the test-based incentives eventually led, around a decade later, to teachers in Atlanta being convicted of racketeering and serving jail sentences as a result of fixing exam results.

Holmström is in many ways a very conventional economist. His Nobel lecture rapidly becomes full of dense mathematics. He believes that, given the right information and incentives, people will make rational decisions.

This is why his conclusion is so startling. He writes:

> One of the main lessons from working on incentive problems for 25 years is that, within firms, high-powered financial incentives can be very dysfunctional and attempts to bring the market inside the firm are generally misguided.

The whole trend in recent years has been to bring even more market-type systems inside companies. For example, managers are often no longer given a budget which they have discretion to spend according to their own judgement and experience. Instead, they have to make a detailed quantitative case to a department which is deemed to have particular expertise in assessing rates of return on spending.

Holmström's conclusion implies the need for a pretty radical rethink of the way incentives are structured, in both the public and private sectors.

26 July 2017

Why teachers are just like bankers

The piece, published five years previously to the one imme-diately above, took up a similar theme of inappropriate in-centive structures leading to undesirable outcomes (Ostrom 1990, 2012).

The summer exam results for school students had just been published. For about the twentieth consecutive year, they showed a rise in average grades. But these wholly im-plausible results did not reflect improved performance from the students. Rather, they arose from the reaction of teachers and exam boards to the performance targets which had been set. Subsequently, the UK government has made changes which have resulted in grade performance starting to fall.

But the fundamental problem of trying to re-develop ap-propriate social norms – which is essentially the focus also of the Holmström paper – rather than rely on incentives and markets in certain contexts still remains at all levels of the UK educational system.

The current highly emotional debate about GCSE grades is not very enlightening. But what has happened tells us a lot about how incentives matter, how they affect outcomes. And at the same time, it shows that unless a proper set of social norms is in place, incentives can have unanticipated, perverse effects. Bankers and teachers have behaved in exactly the same way.

Go back to the major reforms in education under Mrs Thatcher in the 1980s. There is no market within the state sector. So the government tried to mimic the effects of a market by introducing exam targets. Resources for your school in general and your own promotion prospects depended on hitting these targets. Teachers were given an incentive to improve, just like in a real market. Or at least, that was the theory.

Incentives did indeed work, but in an unanticipated way, with an undesirable outcome. Teachers worked out that targets could be met by entering pupils for the more Mickey Mouse subjects. These boomed at the expense of subjects like physics.

Nobel Laureate Elinor Ostrom got her prize for pointing out that markets were not the solution to everything. Social norms, emerging from the interactions between people, can trump incentives. So if the teachers had upheld a set of social norms which disapproved of the devaluation of standards, we would not be in the current mess. But they didn't. Most individual teachers are left wing, but they acted like caricatures of Rational Economic Person in their own self-interest, just like the bankers they despise.

What about the exam boards and grade inflation? No one outside the state education sector believes that the sustained rise in grades over a 24 year period has any real meaning. The boards compete in a real market for students to take their exams. Competition is almost always beneficial. It keeps suppliers on their toes, forcing them to innovate, and improves quality. The concept of wasteful competition is virtually an oxymoron.

But in education, we are dealing not in competing goods and services, but in competing currencies, where a different set of rules apply. The unit of value is the quality of the grades. Collectively, it was in their interests to maintain standards. Individually, each board had an incentive to make the exams that little bit easier. The outcome has been a catastrophic downward spiral in standards.

We have seen a classic example of Gresham's Law, of bad money driving out good. Why choose to enter your students with a board which tries to uphold standards, when another will supply you with more and better grades for the same 'price', the effort you and your students put in.

Michael Gove[5] is trying to enforce a new set of social norms, with the educational sector once more respecting standards. He must not back down.

29 August 2012

CEO compensation and Jamaican demands for reparations: two sides of the same coin

This piece focuses on the dangerous and destructive incentives created when rent seeking[6] is possible (Krueger 1974). It was prompted by a visit to Jamaica by the then British prime minister, David Cameron. He was presented with demands

5   The then Minister of Education.

6   https://www.forbes.com/sites/davidmarotta/2013/02/24/what-is-rent -seeking-behavior/#66fdc734658a

for billions of pounds in reparations for slavery. But chief executives in the West are just as guilty of rent seeking as the Jamaicans.

David Cameron's visit to Jamaica last week led to vociferous demands for the UK to pay the Caribbean island billions of pounds in reparations for slavery. Most people here reacted with predictable eye-rolls and sighs. Slavery was abolished throughout the British Empire in 1833, nearly two centuries ago. Jamaica has been independent since 1962, over fifty years ago. Surely they have had time to sort themselves out and get a decent economy?

There is much to be said for these arguments. In the early 1960s, for example, South Korea was essentially a poor, agricultural society, only one step up the ladder from subsistence-level incomes. Now, it has a dynamic, modern economy with living standards similar to those of the West. Countries such as Singapore have followed similar trajectories.

The demands for payment are a classic example of what economists call 'rent seeking' activity. The word 'rent' here does not mean what you pay on your apartment to live in it. The concept goes all the way back to Adam Smith himself, though the phrase was only coined in the late twentieth century. Rent seeking means trying to increase your share of existing wealth without creating any new wealth.

But we should not feel too much moral superiority over the Jamaicans. Rent seeking has proliferated in Western society in the last couple of decades. The US economy has performed well over this period. Its success is reflected in the amounts paid to CEOs, with the average compensation in the top 350 firms being around \$15 million a year. This enormous sum is some 300 times higher than the amount the companies pay to the typical worker.

In the mid-1970s, the ratio was not 300:1 but only 30:1. Even in the mid-1990s it was around 100:1. This later figure would still hand the average CEO some \$5 million today, not a bad sum to have. It is hard to justify these payments in terms of the contribution the individuals are making to creating new wealth. Some of it, yes, but essentially these pillars of our society have been rent seeking on a grand scale.

Rent seeking by the public sector characterised Gordon Brown's long period as Chancellor. Public spending rose dramatically. But much of the increase did not go to provide better public services. Instead, it paid for the private consumption of those employed in the public sector.

Some graduates in Hollande's France flee abroad. Most of the rest aspire to become a *fonctionnaire*. Good pay, virtually unsackable, and with a gold-plated pension at the end, it is a much sought-after position. Little wonder that France has essentially registered no economic growth since 2011. Jeremy Corbyn eulogised the Italians for subsidising a steel plant rather than letting it go under like Redcar. But rent seeking proliferates in Italy, and their living standards are now back to those of the late 1990s.

Economists disagree about many things, but they are united in their opposition to rent seeking, an unequivocally Bad Thing.

7 October 2015

Corporation tax: fostering the illusions of the electorate that someone else will pay

In the autumn of 2012 Prime Minister David Cameron pronounced himself unhappy with the amounts of corporation tax which large companies such as Starbucks were paying. It remains a political issue to this day. In August 2017, for example, Amazon, perfectly legitimately, not only paid no corporation tax at all, but actually received a small refund from the taxman, despite its UK sales being £7.3 billion.

It is easy to appreciate why this attracts public opprobrium. Many politicians regard tightening up, and even increasing the rates of corporation tax as painless way of raising money. In the 2017 general election, Labour believed that it could raise an additional £19.4 billion in this way.

Leave aside the fact that firms would adjust their behaviour, and the Labour figure is a pure fantasy. Corporation tax is a very bad tax indeed. Ultimately, only individuals can bear tax. The piece describes the different ways in which this can happen

Corporation tax is very much in the news. Starbucks is merely the latest to be in the spotlight, having paid no corporation tax on more than £1 billion of sales in the past three years. This became noteworthy when the prime minister himself declared he was unhappy with the level of tax avoidance by big corporations working in Britain.

The plain fact is that if corporation tax did not exist, it would be madness to introduce it. The tax plays to the ignorance not only of the general public, but of almost all politicians. It encourages the fantasy that there is a free lunch, that someone else will pick up the bill for the welfare state and bloated state bureaucracy.

Mainstream economic theory has many faults, but it is by no means a completely empty box. A key insight is that, ultimately, the tax burden can only fall on individuals. Companies are simply legal entities. If a company pays more corporation tax, someone, somewhere, pays the bill.

There are untold nuances to corporate tax law, what can and cannot be offset and so on. To illustrate the basic economic principles, we need to set these aside. So, for example, one way for a company to respond to an increase in corporation tax is to reduce dividends. Obviously, the income of the shareholders suffers, and these include pension funds. Higher corporation tax might lead to lower pensions.

Another way to respond to an increase in the corporate tax levy is to offset it by holding down wage increases. This way, the company's workforce gets less money. Or the overall wage bill might be reduced by simply not employing as many people. So, somewhere, some people pay the price of the tax by not being offered jobs.

Alternatively, the company could try and be tougher with its suppliers, screwing their prices down. In this case, the supplying companies in general and their workforces pay the cost of the tax. Or capital expenditure plans can be cut back, when the burden falls on the specific group of firms who supply such equipment.

In all these examples, the cost of the increase in corporation tax is eventually borne by individuals. The specific ways in which these actions might be implemented will depend upon the subtleties of the tax system. But there is no escape from the fundamental fact that only people can pay tax.

There is a further cost to the massive complications of current tax law. Highly skilled professionals are employed by HMRC, by big companies and by the major accounting firms solely to do battle over the interpretation of legislation. Abolishing corporation tax would free up these resources for productive uses rather than the complete waste which the current system demands.

Of course, it would be a bold, not to say foolhardy, politician who would make this promise in the current climate. But eventually Western electorates will have to face up to many realities, including the one that corporation tax does them no good.

31 October 2012

Our Friends in the North[7] are trapped in a monetary union

Britain's regional divides have intensified over the past couple of decades. There are sharp differences in prosperity within regions as well. But taking the regions as a whole, London and the South East have leapt ahead of the rest of the country.

Standard international trade theory can help us understand the predicament of the regions. Everywhere in the UK

---

7   This refers to a classic television series of the 1990s, which charts the lives of four friends from the North East from the mid-1960s to the mid-1980s.

is in the sterling monetary union, and the piece describes how a lack of competitiveness in an area manifests itself in a monetary union (McKinnon 1963).

Michael Heseltine's report on economic growth came out last week. It contains 89 recommendations. A mere 57 varieties, to recall the famous Heinz slogan, might have connected it more with popular culture.

The report has already attracted a lot of comment, mainly that Lord Heseltine seems nostalgic for things like the Regional Development Agencies and the decades of the 60s and 70s. The report does at least have the merit of stating a list of possible policy actions to deal with a serious problem.

But what *is* to be done about the regions of the UK? The first thing to note, of course, is that there are very marked differences within each of the individual regions. Towns like Hexham, Harrogate and Wilmslow are every bit as prosperous as the Home Counties. So talking about the problem of the regions is an over-simplification.

Yet the fact remains that there is a problem. Incomes per head are much higher in London and the South East than in any other region taken as a whole, and average unemployment rates are lower. If anything, the gaps are widening over time.

In a nutshell, the regions suffer from the fact that they are in a monetary union with two very dynamic and productive areas, London and the South East. The monetary union in this case is the sterling area. We are not accustomed to think of it in this way. But the underlying problems of Greece and Spain are the same as those of

Yorkshire and Wales. They are uncompetitive in their respective monetary unions.

Britain's regions do not face such acute problems as Euro zone countries, for two reasons. First, they have lacked the autonomy to take decisions which have bankrupted some of the states of Southern Europe. Second, until now, the prosperous South of Britain has been happy to hand over large sums of money to keep the regions afloat.

Essentially, our regions are running large balance-of-payments deficits with London and the South East. They are not sufficiently competitive to produce enough goods and services which we want to buy. In a monetary union, a balance-of-payments deficit translates into lower growth and higher unemployment, something which standard trade theory, one of the best bits of economics, shows clearly.

The coalition's policy of regional pay is therefore a Good Thing. Paradoxically, Britain's regions are poor because they pay themselves too much. They cannot devalue their currency against London to make themselves competitive, so they need to price themselves back into the market.

But they also need more trade, and this means more links, more connections with London and the South East. Modern network theory has been used to provide exciting new perspectives on the structure and patterns of world trade.

The same principles apply within a country. More connections through infrastructure give the regions a chance to transform themselves, and become prosperous areas again, as they were in the nineteenth century, when they led the world.

7 November 2012

Can game theory help the Greeks?

Game theory features strongly in most undergraduate and graduate courses in economics.[8] It rapidly becomes highly mathematical which, if we are being honest, is one of the reasons economists are attracted to it (Mirowski 2001).

There is a deeper reason. In situations such as oligopoly, where there are only a few firms in the market, you must pay attention to the strategies which your competitors follow, at a detailed, individual level. Game theory is a concept which identifies rational strategies to follow in such situations.

It does provide some powerful, general insights. But in most practical situations, it often runs up against the problem that the rules of the game are not always both clear and fixed. The finance minister in the first far left Syriza Greek government, Yanis Varoufakis, was an academic expert in game theory. But it did not do him much good in negotiations with the European Central Bank.

Subsequent to this piece, game theory combined with artificial intelligence has made great progress. For example, in January 2017, a game theoretic algorithm developed by researchers in AI at Carnegie Mellon University won nearly $2 million at poker from four of the world's leading players. Even more impressively, an algorithm developed by the Deep Mind team at Google beat the world champion at the immensely complex game of Go. But in all games of this kind, the rules are fixed. In the real world it's not so simple.

---

8   https://plato.stanford.edu/entries/prisoner-dilemma/

Game theory is a big topic in academic economics. It is scarcely possible to graduate from a good university without exposure to its abstruse logic. So perhaps the Greek government, replete with economists, is using game theory to plan its tactics. Or is Chancellor Merkel herself being briefed with calculations carried out deep in a hidden bunker stuffed with game theorists?

The subject was invented in the 1940s by John von Neumann, one of the greatest polymaths of the entire twentieth century. He made major contributions to the development of both the computer and the atomic bomb. But it is for his game theory that economists remember him. It appears to offer a rational, calculable way of dealing with uncertainty.

The US military poured huge resources into the topic, using some of the best minds in the country, shortly after World War II, once the Soviet Union acquired nuclear weapons.

Both the Americans and the Russians could be assumed to be rational in the sense of preferring to avoid a nuclear exchange. But, lacking certainty about the strategy of the opponent, might the best action be to launch a pre-emptive strike? This is the whole essence of game theory. In the jargon, you either play a cooperative strategy, or you defect. In other words, you either live with the nuclear stand-off, or you get your retaliation in first.

To cooperate or to defect, that is the question. The game being played in the current Greek tragedy is a multi-player one, but the principle is the same. The Greek government hints at a willingness to defect by cosying up to Putin's

Russia, scaring the NATO establishment. From a Greek perspective, the statements of hardliners in, for example, the European Central Bank is equivalent to a policy of defection being played against them. No concessions, according to this strategy.

This fundamental insight of game theory does tell us something about the world. Cartels, for example, are difficult to sustain. Although members benefit by keeping prices up, by playing a cooperative strategy, there is the constant temptation for individuals to defect, to believe that they can steal an advantage by going it alone. Even OPEC has not been immune from this pressure.

Beyond this important general contribution, game theory does not offer much guide in many practical situations. There are now literally tens of thousands of dense mathematical academic papers which try and obtain the optimal strategy. Even the brief bits of English in the articles would be incomprehensible to non-specialists. But the final answer has not yet been found.

Perhaps the biggest weakness is that game theory requires clear and distinct rules of the game. In the current Euro crisis, it is not even clear that the players are in the same game. For Greece, it is a one-off, they want to change policy in their own country. For the ECB, IMF, Germany, if they cooperate in this, the worries are about the next game in the sequence against Spain, Italy or whoever. Politics is a better guide than economics.

4 February 2015

With hurricanes raging, why can't politicians confront climate change?

As noted in the Introduction, microeconomic theory – how individuals make decisions – has made important developments in recent decades. This piece shows how modern theory helps us understand why it is so difficult in practice to tackle climate change (Heal 2017; Laibson 1997).

The devastating storms in America have kept the issue of climate change firmly in the public mind.

But so far, it has proved very difficult for politicians to persuade electorates to change consumption patterns in ways which many scientists would like to see. More expensive air travel, steeper energy bills, these are not very popular.

People are being asked to accept lower increases, or even reductions, in their living standards now, in exchange for escaping potentially large costs in the future.

The problem is easy to state. But it raises some difficult issues in economic theory.

An obvious one is how to analyse uncertainty. Suppose, for example, you are offered odds of four to one on a horse in a particular race. You can then judge whether you think the true probability of it winning is more or less than the odds suggest.

But the uncertainty around the whole climate change issue is much trickier to deal with. It is as if you are offered these odds on a horse, but you do not know which other horses it will be running against.

A simple illustration is given by Geoff Heal of Columbia University in a paper in the latest *Journal of Economic Literature*. We face both scientific and socioeconomic uncertainty. Uncertainty about the underlying science of climate change and uncertainty about the economic and social impacts of an altered climate.

Heal points out that scientists working on climate change take it almost for granted that a rise in global temperature of 2 to 3 degrees would inflict massive costs on our societies. However, he goes on to say that 'nothing in the emerging econometric studies of the impact of climate on economic activity confirms these dramatic concerns'. So even the different groups of experts disagree.

A second challenge is that people value benefits received and costs incurred in the present and the immediate future, more than they do the same amounts in the more distant future.

The Bank of England is rock solid and has never defaulted. So when it issues debt, you can be as certain as possible that you will get your money back. But the Bank still has to offer you interest, more money in the future, to persuade you to buy it now.

A key question is then: How do people discount the future? What rate of interest do they use when they think about it?

Behavioural economics has provided a large amount of evidence on this question. It is not at all good news for climate change activists. In the jargon, people often use 'hyperbolic discounting'. Translated, this simply means they place far more weight on small rewards or costs which occur now than on much larger ones in the more distant future.

A non-obvious implication of this is that they make choices today that their future self would prefer not to have made, despite knowing the same information.

Economics cannot solve the problem of climate change. But it can explain why electorates are so reluctant to do anything about it.

13 September 2017

Ticket prices, fairness and behavioural economics

Liverpool football club announced that there would be a substantial increase in the price of season tickets. This led to general outrage and accusations of profiteering at the expense of the fans.

The top behavioural economist Richard Thaler has given many similar examples (Thaler 2015; Ormerod 2016). He argues that the opposition to 'price gouging' of customers stems not from rational behaviour, but from an inherent sense of fairness.

The piece points out that standard theory makes a clear distinction between short- and long-run profit maximisation by firms. This can explain the Liverpool situation very well, without resource to behavioural economics.

More generally, mainstream economists argue that many of the 'behavioural' situations which are claimed to be identified can be explained perfectly well by standard theory.

Who wants to watch the Scousers[9] play football? Certainly, no Mancunian, and probably no self-respecting Londoner. Yet demand for tickets at Anfield, the home of Liverpool FC, is high. Indeed, there is excess demand. More people want to watch the games than there is room for in the stadium.

In keeping with the precepts of market economics, the owners of the club proposed to increase the price of entry to the ground. From next season, this would rise to a minimum of £77 a game for the Main Stand, up from £59. This provoked a massive walk out of some 10,000 fans from a Liverpool home game, nicely timed to coincide with the game's 77th minute. In response, the owners, Fenway Sports Group, announced last week they were not only withdrawing the proposed increase, but there would now be a two-year price freeze on tickets.

The *Liverpool Echo*, the paper responsible for the memorable 1950s headline about the renowned polar explorer 'Sir Vivian Fuchs Off to the Antarctic', was ecstatic, reflecting the mood of the fans. The manager, Jurgen Klopp, was quoted as saying the price freeze showed that the owners 'really care about the club and the interests of supporters'.

Earlier this month, the Super Bowl between the Carolina Panthers and the Denver Broncos took place in Santa Clara, California. Yet wherever it is played, between whatever teams, this is *the* major event in the American sporting calendar. The price of TV advertising slots reflects the huge interest. It is sky high, and nobody objects to this particular application of basic market principles.

---

9   A demotic expression for an inhabitant of Liverpool. There is a traditional, bitter rivalry with the city of Manchester, barely more than 30 miles away.

The top behavioural economist Richard Thaler, in his recent book *Misbehaving*, argues that the NFL, the sporting body which runs the Super Bowl, takes a different, long-term strategic view towards ticket prices, keeping them reasonable despite huge demand. He quotes an NFL representative saying that this strategy fosters its 'ongoing relationship with fans and business associates'.

Thaler gives a number of examples, in a wide range of non-sporting contexts, in which 'gouging' the customer by reflecting any increase in demand in a price rise, is not seen by the companies as being the best strategy. Being a behavioural economist, he ascribes this to consumers having an inherent sense of 'fairness'. He writes: 'The value of seeming fair should be especially high for firms that plan to be in business selling to the same customers for a long time, since those firms have more to lose from seeming to act unfairly'.

Thaler has worked for over thirty years with the original member of what we might think of as the behavioural economics Hall of Fame – Daniel Kahneman. *Misbehaving* is an important book.

But is much of behavioural economics just mutton dressed as lamb? It is not necessary to invoke the behavioural concept of 'fairness' to explain company behaviour in these examples. Mainstream economics has a long tradition of distinguishing between short- and long-run profit-maximising behaviour. That is all we need to understand pricing at both Anfield and the Super Bowl.

17 February 2016

Are the markets telling the truth?

An important area where behavioural economics has exercised a powerful influence on the mainstream is stock markets. There is strong evidence that, for example, even professional investors exhibit persistent over-confidence. They continue to expect results to be better than they turn out to be.

This article was prompted by large amounts of volatility in financial and commodity markets in the opening month of the year. It draws on the work of Nobel Laureate Robert Shiller, suggesting that financial markets exhibit far too much volatility across both time and place to be compatible with the standard, rational theoretical view of how these markets 'should' behave (Shiller 1981, 2013; Jones 2015).

The opening month of 2016 has been marked by sharp falls in asset prices, not just in financial markets but in commodities such as oil. The conventional wisdom is that the markets form a rational assessment of future prospects for the economy, and set prices accordingly. So if prices fall, we should be downgrading our forecasts for economic growth.

The underlying theory is that shares in any particular company only have value because of the future stream of dividends which the owner of the share will receive. If the outlook for the economy becomes gloomier, the expectation becomes that firms will not make as much profits, and dividend payments will be reduced. So share prices fall.

It sounds plausible. But in recent years, developments within economics have cast serious doubt on whether financial markets are rational in this way. A key player has been Robert Shiller, professor at Yale and winner of the Nobel Prize in 2013. The title of his first paper on the topic, published as long ago as 1981, summarises his argument: 'Do stock prices move too much to be justified by subsequent changes in dividends?'

Shiller looked at data from the 1920s onwards, and showed that stock prices moved up and down to a much greater extent than did dividends. This excess volatility, as he called it, was confirmed when evidence going back into the nineteenth century was examined. If dividends are meant to determine prices, yet shares fluctuate much more, there is clearly something wrong with the theory.

Although his article was published in the top-ranked *American Economic Review*, it was originally widely regarded as a bit weirdo. Gradually, however, as events unfolded like the 20 per cent crash in share prices in a single day in 1987, his arguments became more persuasive.

Recent years have seen developments which reinforce Shiller's point. In February 2015, for example, Brad Jones published an IMF Working Paper on asset bubbles. He points out that the value of globally traded financial assets increased from some $7 trillion in 1980 to around $200 trillion now.

Even more importantly, banks no longer dominate the market. The value of assets under management of investment firms is now nearly as large as that held by the large global banks. People have become richer, are saving more, and look for companies to manage their money.

Jones argues that the incentives facing asset managers lends itself to herding behaviour and excess volatility in the markets. The tyranny of the quarterly report drives decisions. A fund simply cannot risk taking a view which is too contrary to that of the consensus. A manager may eventually be proved correct, but if in the short term loses money, investors will simply pile out of his or her fund.

Ironically, of course, large falls in markets still have the capacity to be self-fulfilling. By destroying the value of wealth, they reduce future spending. Still, it was another Nobel Laureate, Paul Samuelson, who famously remarked that 'the stock market has forecast nine of the last five recessions.'

27 January 2016

The value of experiments, both controlled and natural

Behavioural economics is a good illustration of how at the micro level the discipline has moved forward in recent decades. Even more recently, economists have imported the methodology of randomised controlled trials to evaluate the impact of policy programmes.

But as well as experiments which are designed and controlled, as social scientists we should always be on the lookout for what are termed natural experiments. That is, situations which have arisen naturally, but which allow the contrast between different types of policy to become clear. A major natural experiment has been between the market-oriented economies of the West and centrally planned, socialist ones.[10]

10 https://www.economist.com/news/finance-and-economics/21591573-once-treated-scorn-randomised-control-trials-are-coming-age-random-harvest

A red-hot topic in economics is randomised controlled trials (RCT). Esther Duflo, the MIT academic who has really driven this idea, has surely put herself in pole position for a Nobel Prize at some point.

The idea of RCTs has been imported from medicine. One group of people are selected at random to be subject to a particular policy, and the outcomes in this set are compared to the rest of the population, which are not.

The studies have been almost exclusively carried out in developing countries. Evaluating RCTs often involves some subtle statistical points, but they are a powerful way of identifying what really works. Their policy impact has already been substantial.

Over 200 million people worldwide have been reached by the scaling up of programmes evaluated by the J-PAL network in which Duflo is the leading light. The RCT studies themselves are carried out on a small scale, evaluating very particular policies. If they succeed, they can be expanded. Examples include encouraging the take-up of school-based deworming, chlorine dispensers for safe water and free insecticidal bed nets.

A closely related concept is known as a natural experiment. This is when we observe two contrasting policies which have been carried out in the past, either at the same time on different populations or at different times on the same one.

The policies in this case have not been deliberately designed as part of an experiment. They have been introduced as part of the political process.

But good natural experiments can be just as informative as RCTs. Indeed, they can reach the parts which RCTs cannot get to, because we can observe natural experiments which have taken place on very large scales.

By far the most important of these is the series of natural experiments on the performance of market-oriented economies compared to their centrally planned socialist rivals.

The current tensions highlight the differences between North and South Korea. In the 1950s, the latter had living standards similar to African countries. Now, they are at Western levels. Other countries which were poor in the mid-twentieth century and which have adopted the principles of market-oriented economics have also prospered.

The fall of the Berlin Wall at the end of the 1980s brought into sharp focus the contrast between East and West Germany. The Trabant was a popular car in the East. But it was of such poor quality that its value dropped to almost zero as soon as Western cars could be imported.

The major economic contest of the twentieth century was between the US and the Soviet Union, won easily by America.

India and China practised different forms of socialism until the late 1980s. The Chinese was the most extreme and resulted, for example, in the deaths of at least 60 million people in the self-induced famines around 1960. After adopting market principles, both countries have flourished.

The outcomes of these major natural experiments are decisive. Belief in socialism in 2017 is equivalent to believing the Sun goes round the Earth.

4 October 2017

Rude Yorkshiremen, Milton Friedman and economic theory

Even apparently mundane events are replete with important aspects of economic theory. This piece was prompted by a story of a bookseller in Yorkshire who was exceptionally rude to his prospective customers which featured prominently in that week's newspapers.

One of the issues this raised is the timescale over which responses to incentives take place. In principle, the bookseller would be forced out of business because of the low quality of his offer (Friedman 1962). Most people prefer not be on the receiving end of abuse. But the processes of theory, while they describe the eventual outcome accurately, may take a long time to unfold (Atkinson 1969).

As it happens, in this case the bookseller did give up only a few months after the piece was written. But it is not clear that this was solely due to lack of custom, it seems that he himself may have become the target of abuse locally.

A bookseller in the Yorkshire Dales was in the headlines last week. He called a customer a 'pain in the arse', and has been the subject of numerous complaints to the local parish council about his rudeness. To complete the outrage, he charges 50p as entry fee to his shop.

The incident is at face value simply an amusing and trivial story. But it raises interesting issues in economic theory.

In principle, if the bookseller kept on offending potential customers, he would be driven out of business by market forces. People would no longer use his shop, and would take their custom elsewhere.

In a much more important context, Milton Friedman made a very similar argument about racial discrimination in employment in the US. In the process of hiring, Friedman believed that a profit-maximising company would always choose the best person for the job, regardless of his or her background. To do otherwise would impose unnecessary costs on the firm, and it would be driven out of business by its non-discriminatory competitors.

Discrimination of all kinds does appear to be much lower in capitalist economies than under other forms of social and economic organisation. But it is not at all clear how much of this is directly due to market forces.

Economic theory focuses on equilibrium, the situation which notionally exists when all the various incentives, costs, profits and so on have worked their way through the system.

But economics says very little about both the process by which equilibrium is reached, and how long it takes to get there. A very distinguished British economist, Tony Atkinson, died last week. A brilliant paper he published when in his early 20s showed that in the core model of growth in economic theory, moving from one equilibrium to another would take over 100 years.

In practice, market forces do work. But they are an imperfect filter of firms' evolutionary fitness to survive. Numerous studies show that the most efficient firms in an industry often record productivity levels three or four times higher than the least efficient. And these differences persist. Inefficient companies can survive for a long time.

The 50p entry fee, refunded if a purchase is made, raises a further issue for economics. The shop is next to a bus stop, and the owner believed that many browsers were simply taking refuge from the wind and rain, with no intention of buying.

So the proprietor was simply creating a market. In this case, proper shelter and warmth for bus travellers. But the entry fee generated general outrage. This is clearly not an area in which the use of markets is believed to be appropriate.

The same sentiment is behind the otherwise inexplicable support for a return to state ownership of railways. Anyone who can remember British Rail will shudder at the memory of just how awful it was. Yet, like health, many believe that it is not morally correct to use markets in this context.

Economics and experts are under attack. But economics can illuminate many aspects of everyday life.

18 January 2017

Banks and steel: thorny problems in economic theory

It was announced that some major steel plants in the UK were under threat of closure, with devastating short-term effects on their local economies. This article considers the question: if the bankers could be bailed out, why not steel?

This is perhaps the most difficult piece in the book (Duffie and Sonnenschein 1989). For the simple question raises a fundamental issue in economic theory. Why is money important? The answer given may seem esoteric. Further, it is not one which many mainstream economists would subscribe to. Money is important because it is the only commodity which appears in all markets.

The potential closure of the Tata steel plants, and the plight of Port Talbot, is a tragedy for those directly affected. A key question is: if the banks could be saved, why not steel? From a purely political perspective, the topic has legs. The loyal, hardworking Welshmen, fearful for their families' futures, contrasted with the arrogant pin-striped bankers, ripping everyone off. It is a difficult narrative for the government to counter.

Away from the hurlyburly of politics, the challenge takes us to some issues at the very heart of economic theory. Economics for beginners starts off with a simple diagram showing how much firms would supply of a product at different prices, and how much consumers would demand. The point where these two curves cross tells us the price which exactly balances supply with demand. In the technical phrase, the market clears.

A fundamental question in economics has been whether it is possible to prove that a set of prices can be found which would clear every single market, creating what economists call 'general equilibrium'. Supply and demand would be in balance everywhere, and so there would be no unused resources. It is a problem which is easy to state, but exceptionally hard to prove. No less than seven out of the first eleven Nobel Prizes were awarded for work in this area.

Readers may recall having to solve quadratic equations at school. It has been proved that there is a formula which solves every such equation. Plug in the numbers, and out pops the answer. The general equilibrium problem is similar, but at a much harder mathematical level. Can some formula, as we can think of it, be found which proves that a set of prices can be found for every economy?

The work may be esoteric, but it has great practical influence. Much of regulatory policy, for example, is designed to try and remove impediments to the workings of markets, to try and bring about the desired state of general equilibrium, where all resources are fully utilised.

A crucial problem for this work, in many ways the crown jewel of economic theory, is that it has proved very hard to establish that money has any special significance. It is simply another commodity. This thorny theoretical issue was highlighted by the financial crisis, which the mainstream equilibrium models could not explain. In essence, both money and steel are equally as important. Economists will realise I am compressing points here, but in this framework if the banks can be saved so, too, can steel.

Economists not obsessed with equilibrium, like Keynes, often take a completely different view. Money is decisively different, because it is the only product which appears in every single market. Disruptions to money are not confined to a particular part of the economy, but have an impact everywhere.

Milton Friedman believed that the Great Recession in America in the 1930s had a monetary explanation for this very reason. Money is fundamentally different to steel. The banks had to be saved, steel is just an option.

6 April 2016

Expert opinions are often built on sand

This piece serves as a link into the next section of the book, which is on the limits to knowledge. There has been a huge increase in recent years in the number of papers published in academic journals. But, especially in the social sciences and health, this has led to very few genuine insights.[11] Incentives and economic theory help us understand why this is the case.

Last week we saw yet another major reversal of opinion by experts. For years we have all been lectured severely on the need to finish every single course of prescription drugs. But the latest wisdom is that this is not necessary

The announcement that petrol and diesel cars will be banned by 2040 only serves to remind the millions of diesel car owners that they were told only a few years ago that diesel was a Good Thing.

These stories have been very prominent in the media. But they are by no means isolated examples. Such reversals of opinion are all too common in the softer social and medical sciences. The 'evidence base', a phrase beloved of metropolitan liberal experts, is often built on sand.

This is neatly illustrated by psychology. *Science* is probably the most prestigious scientific journal in the world. At the end of 2015, a group of no fewer than 270 authors published a paper in it. They were all part of the teams which had published 100 scientific articles in top psychology journals.

---

11 For example, *Science*, 28 August 2015, http://science.sciencemag.org/con tent/349/6251/aac4716

In only 16 out of the 100 cases could the experimental results be replicated sufficiently closely to be confident that the original finding was valid.

The papers had been published in top psychology journals, and the original authors were involved in the replication experiment. So the replication rate should have been high. Instead, it was so low that the lead author of the *Science* piece points out that they effectively knew nothing. The original finding could be correct, the different result in the attempted replication could be. Or neither of these could be true.

There is no suggestion at all that any sort of fraud or misrepresentation was involved when the original results were submitted for publication.

But economic theory helps us understand how this situation came about. The great insight of economics is that people react to incentives.

Academics now face immense pressure to publish research papers. If they do not, they get more burdensome teaching loads, don't get promoted and might even get sacked. Their incentive is to publish.

Academic journals will only very rarely accept a paper which contains negative results. The whole culture is to find positive ones. So experiments will be re-designed, run with different samples, until that sought-after positive finding is obtained.

More and more academics are now desperate to publish more and more papers. To meet this increase in demand, there has been a massive increase in the supply of journals willing to publish. Many of these are highly dubious, being prepared to accept papers on payment of a fee by the authors.

For all except a small elite of individuals and institutions, academic life has become increasingly proletarianised. In the old Soviet Union, workers could get medals for exceeding the quota of, say, boot production. It did not matter if all the boots were left footed.

Many universities are now similar, with useless articles being churned out to meet the demands of bureaucrats. Time for a big purge, both of academics and their institutions.

2 August 2017

References

Adda, J. and Cornaglia, F. (2006) Taxes, cigarette consumption and smoking intensity. *American Economic Review* 96: 1013–28 (https://www.gov.uk/government/publications/sugar-reduction-from-evidence-into-action).

Allcott, H. and Rogers, T. (2014) The short-run and long-run effects of behavioral interventions: experimental evidence from energy conservation. *American Economic Review* 104(10): 3003–37.

Atkinson, A. B. (1969) The timescale of economic models: how long is the long-run? *Review of Economic Studies* 36(2): 137–52.

Dolton, P. and Vignoles, A. (2000) The incidence and effects of overeducation in the U.K. graduate labour market. *Economics of Education Review* 19: 179–98.

Drago, F., Galbiati, R. and Vertova, P. (2009) The deterrent effects of prison: evidence from a natural experiment. *Journal of Political Economy* 117(2): 257–80.

Duffie, D. and Sonnenschein, H. (1989) Arrow and general equilibrium theory. *Journal of Economic Literature* 27(2): 565–98.

Friedman, M. (1962) *Capitalism and Freedom.* University of Chicago Press.

Heal, G. (2017) The economics of the climate. *Journal of Economic Literature* 55(3): 1046–63.

Holmström, B. (2017) Pay for performance and beyond. *American Economic Review* 107(7): 1753–77.

Humphrey, T. H. (1996) The early history of the box diagram (https://www.richmondfed.org/~/media/richmondfedorg/publications/research/economic_quarterly/1996/winter/pdf/history.pdf).

Jones, B. (2015) Asset bubbles: re-thinking policy for the age of asset management, IMF Working Paper (http://www.imf.org/external/pubs/ft/wp/2015/wp1527.pdf).

Krueger, A. (1974) The political economy of the rent-seeking society. *American Economic Review* 64(3): 291–303.

Laibson, D. (1997) Golden eggs and hyperbolic discounting. *Quarterly Journal of Economics* 112(2): 443–77.

Levitt, S. and Dubner, S. J. (2005) *Freakonomics: A Rogue Economist Explores the Hidden Side of Everything.* New York: William Murrow.

McKinnon, R. I. (1963) Optimum currency areas. *American Economic Review* 53(4): 717–25.

Mirowski, P. (2001) *Machine Dreams: Economics Becomes a Cyborg Science.* Cambridge University Press.

Ormerod, P. (2016) Picking up the gauntlet: Richard Thaler's defence of behavioural economics. *Economic Affairs*, DOI: 10.1111/ecaf.12159.

Ostrom, E. (1990) *Governing the Commons: The Evolution of Institutions for Collective Action.* Cambridge University Press.

Ostrom, E. (2009) Beyond markets and states: polycentric governance of complex economic systems. Nobel Prize lecture, December (https://www.nobelprize.org/nobel_prizes/ecomic-sciences/laureates/2009/ostrom_lecture.pdf).

Ostrom, E. (2012) *The Future of the Commons: Beyond Market Failure & Government Regulations.* Institute of Economic Affairs: Occasional Papers. (https://iea.org.uk/publications/research/the-future-of-the-commons-beyond-market-failure-and-government-regulation).

Raw, C., Page, B. and Hodgson, G. (1971) *Do You Sincerely Want to Be Rich? The Full Story of Bernard Cornfeld and IOS.* New York:

Viking Press. (http://www.parliament.uk/documents/bank ing-commission/banking-final-report-volume-i.pdf).

Shiller, R. (1981) Do stock prices move too much to be justified by subsequent changes in dividends? *American Economic Review* 71(3): 421–36.

Shiller, R. (2013) Nobel Prize lecture (https://www.nobelprize .org/nobel_prizes/economic-sciences/laureates/2013/shiller -lecture.pdf.

Smith, V. (2002) Constructivist and ecological rationality in economics, Nobel Prize Lecture, December, https://www.nobel prize.org/nobel_prizes/economic-sciences/laureates/2002/ smith-lecture.pdf).

Stiglitz, J. E. (2001) Information and the change in the paradigm in economics. Nobel Prize lecture, December (https://www .nobelprize.org/nobel_prizes/economic-sciences/laureates/ 2001/stiglitz-lecture.pdf).

Thaler, R. H. (2015) *Misbehaving: The Making of Behavioral Economics*. New York: W. W. Norton.

3 UNCERTAINTY AND THE LIMITS TO KNOWLEDGE

All scientific theories are approximations to reality. In some cases they offer exceptionally accurate representations of reality. But the two are never exactly the same. Even in quantum physics, there are discrepancies between the theory and the world.

In order to understand the world, theories make simplifying assumptions. A key question for any theory is how reasonable these assumptions are.

Economics is essentially a theory of individual behaviour, of how agents – to use the jargon word of economics – choose between alternatives in any given context. This is not meant to be an economics textbook, so this is not the place to discuss all the assumptions made by theory of the Rational Economic Person.

The focus of this section of the book is on one particular aspect of the assumptions. This is the simplifications which are made in economic theory about the ability to gather and process information about the alternatives which are available in any given situation.

For a long time after economic theory first began to be formalised in the late nineteenth century, it was assumed that agents had complete information about the alternatives when they made their choice. The assumption, as readers will know from their own experience, is rarely totally correct. But in many contexts, it is a sufficiently good approximation to reality for it to be useful.

For example, washing machines are at one level a rather neat and sophisticated piece of technology which have removed a lot of drudgery from housework. But at another, they are pretty simple. A buyer does not need to know the science of how the machine operates. He or she just needs a few pieces of information: price, size, colour, brand and the functions which it performs. Even in pre-internet days, it was sufficiently easy to get enough information when considering purchasing a washing machine for the assumption of complete information to be a reasonable one.

Economics has moved forward. As discussed in the Introduction, following the seminal work of George Akerlof and Joe Stiglitz, the everyday toolkit of economists has been extended to allow for the possibility that agents have incomplete information and, indeed, that different agents (e.g. firms) might have quite different amounts of information than others (e.g. consumers).

From a scientific perspective, this development has been very important. It widens dramatically the situations in which the simplifying assumptions of economic theory offer reasonable approximations to reality.

Equipped with these and other advances in microeconomics in recent decades, economics has come to occupy a completely dominant position in the process of policymaking. In 1964, the newly elected Labour government increased the number of professional economists in the civil service to around a dozen. Now, there are 1,400 working across government, not counting those in the central bank and the various massive regulatory bodies. A great deal of policy is filtered through the lens of 'rational' economics before it can be deemed acceptable.

But when decisions made today have potentially important consequences into the future, questions are certainly posed about how far the rational choice model is a good approximation of reality.

Many decisions which agents make, it should be emphasised, do not have important consequences for the future. In a weekly supermarket shop, if you buy a flavour of soup which it turns out you don't like, you can get a different one next week. It is all part of the process of gathering information on alternatives.

But whom should you marry? How much should you put into a pension and, once you have decided, which scheme should you choose? You may very well not make the optimal decision. Indeed, it will not become apparent for many years whether you have even made a tolerably good one.

Decisions which have important consequences into the future suffer from this inherent lack of information. Shareholders in the Briansk Rail and Engineering company had every reason to be pleased in 1912. Their company became ranked in the top 100 of the world's largest commercial firms. Yet, after the Bolsheviks seized power just five years later, not only were their shares expropriated, they were fortunate if they escaped the labour camps and execution cellars.

Keynes, a much more sophisticated thinker than many of his present-day followers realise, was at pains to stress the limits to knowledge about the future in his great 1936 book, *The General Theory of Interest, Employment and Money*.

There are many quotes which would illustrate the point, but one will suffice:

> [T]he outstanding fact is the extreme precariousness of the basis of knowledge on which our estimates of prospective yield [of a new investment] have to be made ... If we speak frankly, we have to admit that our basis of knowledge for estimating the yield 10 years hence of a railway, a copper mine, a textile factory, the goodwill of a patent medicine, an Atlantic liner, a building in the City of London amounts to little and sometimes to nothing.

Hayek, Keynes's great rival, took quite different views to Keynes on a range of issues. The two engaged in major intellectual battles. But Hayek, too, was convinced of the inherent limits to knowledge in economic and social systems. He believed that no amount of cleverness could overcome them.

Even more than Keynes, Hayek made this a central feature of his life's work. His 1974 Nobel Prize lecture was entitled 'The Pretence of Knowledge'.[1] Hayek regarded modern economies as enormously complex systems. Millions of

---

1   https://www.nobelprize.org/nobel_prizes/economic-sciences/laureates/1974/hayek-lecture.html

agents are all making decisions about the future. It would be scarcely credible for all these plans to be compatible with each other. And it would be scarcely credible for someone to predict the outcome arising from these different plans.

At a time when economics is far more important than ever in policymaking, many of its practitioners appear to have forgotten the lessons of Keynes and Hayek. A strong belief permeates the regulatory bodies, finance ministries and central banks around the world. It is the belief that they are sufficiently clever to design rules and regulations which will produce optimal outcomes in the future. If a set of regulations proves inadequate, the answer is almost invariably to design an even more complicated array. This time round, we will surely get it right!

Ironically, during the decades in which the market-oriented capitalist economies demonstrated their decisive superiority over their socialist rivals, the mentality of the central planner grew dramatically in importance among bureaucrats in the West.

The articles in this section are all meant to remind us of the limits to knowledge.

The World Chess Championship tells us
how we really make decisions

An enthralling battle for the world chess championship was taking place. The piece introduces the work of Herbert Simon, a truly brilliant American polymath whose key writings came out in the 1950s and 1960s. Like Keynes and Hayek, Simon was acutely aware of the limits to knowledge. His perspective was subtly different from theirs, and we will meet him again in the section of the book on networks (Simon 1955).

The World Chess Championship is under way. The current champion, the Indian Viswanathan Anand, trails his young rival Magnus Carlsen, by 3 – 5. Carlsen, in the opinion of many, is set fair to become the strongest ever human player. The match is an absorbing spectacle.

But the game of chess is not just interesting in its own right. It tells us a great deal about the nature of the environment in which individuals and firms make decisions, and how these decisions are actually made. Herbert Simon, possibly the greatest social scientist of the second half of the twentieth century, used chess to illustrate his key ideas about decision making.

Simon won the Nobel Prize in economics. He received the Turing Award for his contributions to artificial intelligence and the American Psychological Association conferred on him their Award for Outstanding Lifetime Contributions to Psychology. His day job, as it were, was as professor of industrial management at Carnegie Mellon.

Simon believed that the way in which economists assume people take decisions was profoundly wrong. Rational Economic Person gathers large amounts of information on the alternative choices available in any particular situation, compares them to his or her preferences, and then makes the best possible decision, the 'optimal' as economists say. Simon argued that, in most situations, the environment is so complex that the optimal decision can never be known. Instead, we use what he called 'rules of thumb', simple rules which give reasonably satisfactory outcomes – until they do not!

This is not merely of academic interest. The models of the economy in both finance ministries and central banks are based on the concept of rational decision making. A great deal of regulatory activity is designed to correct what economists see as deviations from 'rational' behaviour, both by consumers and firms.

The game of chess is in principle very simple. There are about a dozen rules, which can be learned easily. The object of the game is unequivocal: to capture the opponent's king. And you know everything which your opponent has done.

But in most situations in the game, the optimal move cannot be computed. Many bad options can be eliminated, and players like Carlsen will do this much more effectively than an average player. Even at world championship level, this is how most games are lost and won. It is not often a matter of superior rational calculation of the consequences of a move. It is the judgement about what constitutes a good move.

Do computers help? All positions with 6 pieces have now been solved. But there are 32 pieces in chess, and the computational complexity scales super-exponentially with the addition of each piece.

The environment in which firms operate is enormously more complicated than the game of chess. Competitors, for example, can innovate and invent entirely new pieces and new rules. We live in a world which is radically uncertain, in which, as Keynes once remarked, 'we have, as a rule, only the vaguest idea of any but the most direct consequences of our acts'.

20 November 2013

The 'gentleman in Whitehall' does not know best

In early 2014, the Conservative–Lib Dem coalition relaxed the very tight restrictions which had been in place regarding people's ability to withdraw sums of money from their pension pots. This drew the wrath of metropolitan liberal commentators, essentially on the grounds that individuals did not know what they were doing and might make wrong decisions. They, the liberal elite, knew what was good for them.

Gordon Brown was Chancellor of the Exchequer – the finance minister – between 1997 and 2007, and prime minister 2007–10. Perhaps no politician of recent years has believed more than Brown that experts like himself really do know best (though the competition has been steep). He even went so far as to claim that he had 'abolished boom and bust' – before the financial crisis!

This gives just a few examples of where the Great Helmsman himself made devastatingly bad decisions during his time as Chancellor.

The government is relaxed about people cashing in their pension schemes to buy a Lamborghini. But the left-leaning liberal commentariat is certainly not. Abuse has been heaped onto George Osborne's Budget measure of removing the requirement for people to buy an annuity. The main thrust of the attacks is that individuals may act irresponsibly. They may take financial decisions that are not in their best interests.

This is certainly true. People do make mistakes. The 1945 Labour government used the infamous phrase, 'The gentleman in Whitehall knows best'. The concept has since been extended to include ladies, and, despite its antiquity, is still very much alive and kicking. This view of the world lies at the heart of the criticisms of Osborne's innovation. But does the state itself have a better track record when it comes to questions of finance? The answer is plain. An entire issue of this newspaper could be filled with shocking decisions. So just a few recent examples will suffice.

The issue of Gordon Brown's disastrous sale of half the UK's gold reserves over the 1999–2002 period was raised last week at prime minister's questions. The average price of our gold was $275 an ounce, and of course the price now stands at some $1,300. Hindsight can make geniuses of us all. But the ineptitude of the process itself was breathtaking. The large sale was announced in advance, on 7 May 1999. This public declaration of a large increase in supply coming on to the market was sufficient to drive the price down 10 per cent by the time the first tranche was auctioned two months later.

The Private Finance Initiative is placing major strains on the finances of the NHS. The concept was created under John Major, but Gordon Brown really loved it. PFIs allowed ministers to secure large sums to invest in popular projects, such as new schools and hospitals, without paying any money up front. The insane financing structure places a debt on the taxpayer which is roughly double the value of the infrastructure which the framework helped to build.

Not everything is Gordon Brown's fault. In the 2010 Strategic Defence Review, the new government announced that they would adopt the aircraft carrier version of the American F35 fighter, rather than the 'jump jet' favoured by the previous Labour administration. But the costs of adapting the design for use on carriers spiralled out of control, and two years later, it was abandoned and the jump jet reinstated.

But who can forget that Brown boasted that he had 'abolished boom and bust'? The Treasury and the thousands of officials in regulatory bodies such as the Financial Services Authority thought they were so clever that they had designed a system in which recessions would never happen. The cost of the crisis can be reckoned not in billions but trillions.

Hayek won the Nobel Prize for his work on the inherent limits to knowledge of economic systems. Individuals, governments, central banks all face these limits. Osborne is right to trust the people.

9 April 2014

How expert are experts? Time to end the independence of the Bank

One of the first decisions which Gordon Brown took as Chancellor in 1997 was to make the Bank of England independent. It was a very fashionable opinion at the time within mainstream academic macroeconomics. This piece examines the record of the Bank's macroeconomic expertise, and finds it wanting.[2]

The Bank of England has held short-term interest rates very close to zero for several years, with devastating consequences for the incomes of millions of frugal people. The Bank's latest wheeze suggests that savers pay the banks for the privilege of holding their money. The Bank has pumped hundreds of billions of pounds into the economy through quantitative easing.

All these policies are open to question. For example, quantitative easing has many critics among distinguished monetary economists.

Despite this, the actions of the Bank are deemed to be a Good Thing, for the Bank is independent. The decisions of its experts are untainted by the touch of mortal, corrupt politicians. Yet just how expert is its expertise?

In 2007, the Bank plotted its 'fan charts' around its central forecast of GDP growth in the UK over the next five years. These show the range of uncertainty the Bank

---

2   http://www.bankofengland.co.uk/publications/Documents/inflation report/ir07nov.pdf, especially chart 5.1 and the discussions on debt.

attaches to the central projection, which is plotted in lines which fan out around it. The further ahead the forecast, the greater the range of uncertainty. So these lines look like a fan on the chart.

According to these charts, there was, for all practical purposes, a zero probability of a recession in the UK during the period 2007–12. Scarcely a year after they were published, the UK entered its deepest recession since the 1930s.

When the crisis struck, the Governor appeared paralysed by the weight of his academic knowledge. As capitalism itself teetered on the brink of disintegration, he spoke of the 'moral hazard' of bailing out banks, seemingly oblivious to the real and massive dangers of banks collapsing in a cascade of failures, like so many dominoes.

The Bank was granted its independence by Gordon Brown. Regrettably, George Osborne imitated him by assigning the economic forecasts of the Treasury to the independent Office for Budget Responsibility. At least Robert Chote, the director of the OBR, is under no illusions that independence somehow ensures his forecasts will be more accurate.

Brown eulogised and revered the cult of the expert, not just at the Bank but across a whole range of social and economic policies. Mere politicians, let alone ordinary voters, are deemed incapable of participating in discussions unless they are familiar with the latest piece of multiple regression analysis waved by an expert bearing a clipboard.

If the experts had genuine expertise, this would be perfectly reasonable. It makes good sense to let an engineer design a bridge. But the level of real understanding in the social sciences – including economics – is very much lower than most experts care to admit. It is no accident that Hayek remarked: 'in the design of successful policies, the role of intellect is grossly exaggerated'.

The time has come to get rid of the insidious cult of the expert, to end the independence of the Bank and to restore decisions to democratically elected politicians. If they get it wrong, at least we can have the pleasure of kicking them out.

6 March 2013

Beer, evolution and failure

There has been an explosion in the past few years of craft beers. Usually with very distinctive flavours and with a high alcohol content, they have become popular with young urban professionals. From very modest beginnings of making just a few barrels a week, three craft breweries in the UK (the latest of which was BrewDog) had been snapped up by the majors for large sums of money.

The piece uses the craft beer market to make the more general point that the success or failure of individual companies is extremely difficult to predict in advance. All firms have an incentive not to fail, and large firms devote a lot of resources to trying to plan for the future. But they still succumb. I draw a parallel between firm evolution and the process of biological evolution, the latter of course being purely random and hence impossible to predict. I expanded on this at considerable length in my book Why Most Things Fail (Ormerod 2005).

Is setting up a micro brewery a licence to print money? This month, a private equity company acquired 22 per cent of BrewDog for just over £200 million, netting a neat £100 million for the founders. Last year, the owners of Budweiser, AB InBev, bought Camden Town Brewery for a reported £85 million. This follows the sale of Meantime Brewery in 2015 to the global giant SAB Miller for an undisclosed amount.

There has been an explosion in the number of craft beer startups. The number of micro breweries in the UK has grown from 1,026 to around 1,700.

But far from replicating the BrewDogs of this world, most of these will fail.

The same thing happens in every innovative market where new products are developed. Between 1900 and 1920 there were almost 2,000 firms involved in automobile production in the US. Over 99 per cent of them disappeared. Before World War I, the European film industry operated on a global scale, supplying half the American market. By 1920, European films had virtually disappeared from the US and had become marginal in Europe itself. Hollywood had taken over.

Being big offers no guarantee against failure. Only this month for example, we have seen the reputation of United Airlines seriously damaged, and Toshiba has projected that its losses this year could be as much as $9 billion. Between 2005 and 2009, MySpace was the largest social networking site in the world. NewsCorp bought it for $580 million in 2005, but sold it in 2011 for just $35 million.

These firms, including MySpace, remain in business for the moment, but many giant companies go under eventually. The failure rate of small businesses is high in the first two or three years of life, because of elementary mistakes such as, for example, not making provision to pay the tax authorities. But, after that, the probabilities of failure in any given year of small and large firms become very similar.

The basic reason is that there is an inherent level of uncertainty about the future, which no amount of cleverness can reduce. In 1914 Briansk Rail and Engineering in Russia was one of the largest industrial companies in the world. But it disappeared in 1917 after the seizure of power by the then tiny Bolshevik Party. This itself became the giant Communist Party of the Soviet Union until it, too, eventually collapsed.

In the economics textbooks, running a business is easy. One of the basic things which students learn is how to maximise the profits of a firm. Even the more advanced material is set in an essentially static world.

The distinguishing features of capitalism are innovation and evolution, but economics has very little to say about these. Things do not just stand still. Last year, for example, Ford had a global income of $151 billion and Tesla had $7 billion. Yet this month, Tesla's market capitalisation has overtaken Ford's.

By all means take early retirement to brew the beer you have always wanted. But don't expect to get rich.

19 April 2017

Ninja Turtles, Nick Clegg and market failure

Staying with the commercial world, we look here at the problem of predicting which toy will become the number 1 Christmas best seller. There are massive uncertainties involved, not least because as Christmas approaches, the market leader will get positive feedback. More children will want it, not because of its inherent attributes, but simply because of the fact that other people have already bought it (Arthur 1994, 1996).

Economic theory does contain models which can handle this sort of behaviour, and they are different from the standard model of rational choice. But markets such as this are becoming more and more widespread in the real world.

The piece contains a paragraph poking fun at two leading members of the Liberal Democrat party in the then coalition government, Nick Clegg and Vincent Cable. Far from being liberal in the traditional, free market sense, many current members of the Lib Dem party in the UK are among the most fervent believers in the supremacy of the 'expert' and in the ability of governments to plan the future successfully.

Christmas is coming. Retailers are beginning to push their offers hard. The first page of a search on Google for 'Christmas Toys 2012' is full of sites announcing the ones which will be 'hot' or 'top'. In total, there are over 75 million results available to be perused.

Last year it was Mishling Tree Monsters, Doggie Doo, and the like which proved the most popular. Readers of a certain age will recall such stupendous commercial triumphs as Teletubbies, Buzz Lightyear and Teenage Mutant Ninja Turtles.

Fond though these memories might be, the runaway successes bring tears as well as joy. Every year, the cult toys of the year become hard, or even impossible, to acquire as the great day approaches.

Perhaps we should look to Nick Clegg and Vince Cable for inspiration, for a pledge to eliminate the failure to anticipate trends. Market short-termism is spoiling Christmas for many of our poorest and most excluded citizens. Reform of the House of Lords and of the voting system itself are an integral part of the change of mindset required to combat the Christmas toy shortage. An urgent review must be undertaken of measures which will prevent shortages arising in future, including legislation to force the banks to lend.

Or is there something deeper involved? Uncertainty is in fact inherent in industries in which fashion plays an important part. The film industry is an obvious example. Even the presence of big stars and huge advertising budgets is no guarantee of success. If the first wave of audiences does not like a big release, the information will spread rapidly, and the studio will be left with a flop, like the $200 million loss-maker *John Carter* earlier this year. Similarly, low-budget movies can become hits.

Markets such as those for films or for Christmas toys raise serious problems for conventional, economic theory. In the orthodox theory of consumer behaviour, the tastes of individuals are given; and the market acts to communicate them to producers, so that appropriate quantities of the relevant product can be supplied.

But when a new release or product is issued by the film or Christmas toy industries it is not subject to given tastes. Consumers do not know in advance whether they will like it or loathe it. In the case of toys, this produces a problem for buyers from the retail chains who are trying to second-guess preferences which are not yet formed. Further, one consumer's attitude depends critically on another's. Your child wants the number 1 toy because every other child wants it too. As soon as such preferences do begin to emerge, they can compound with great speed and leave producers lagging behind.

The world as a whole is becoming less like the economics textbooks and more like Ninja Turtles. Think of the clamour for Apple's iPhone 5. Policymakers in both the public and private sectors need to alter their mindsets to cope.

3 October 2012

Black Friday, games and the Stock Market

Another aspect of commercial uncertainty is discussed here, namely what has become known in a retail context as Black Friday. The term has a number of applications, but in retail it refers to the massive crush in shopping malls and high streets which usually builds up on a particular Friday a few weeks ahead of Christmas. In 2015, even a few days beforehand, dire predictions were being made of the forthcoming mayhem in retail outlets. But in the event, it proved to be a fairly normal Friday.

Black Friday, and events like it, can be analysed using something called the minority game. Developed by two physicists, it is easy to state the rules, and extraordinarily difficult to play. Thousands of academic papers have been written on it, using very difficult maths. But despite this effort, no one has yet come up with the 'best' strategy to play. The optimal rational strategy has not been discovered (Challet et al. 2005).

Black Friday has come and gone. The massive surge into the shops which was anticipated in much of the media failed to materialise. Many retail outlets were quieter than a normal Friday. In contrast, internet shopping went wild. Amazon had its biggest-ever day in the UK, selling over seven million items. Argos and John Lewis experienced problems with their websites because of the huge number of visitors. For the first time ever, online sales are believed to have exceeded £1 billion in a single day.

Experiences such as this raise fundamental questions about the predictability of many social and economic events. The Office for Budget Responsibility handed George Osborne an extra £27 billion to play with in his Autumn Statement by revising its forecasts through to 2020. Many commentators have pointed to the large amount of uncertainty which surrounds them. But these are predictions over a five-year horizon. Even just a week ago, many believed that the shops would be packed on Friday. The retailers themselves geared up for the crush. But it did not happen.

It is always possible after an event to rationalise it. On Black Friday 2014, in an Asda store, shoppers trampled each other and fights broke out as they attempted to grab bargains. This mayhem was publicised widely. Looking back surely it is obvious that this is why people went online rather than risk a repeat of last year's chaos? In fact, hindsight bias, to give it its technical name, appears to be deeply rooted in our individual psychologies.

Something happens, and we often come to believe that it was inevitable. But this is not what the retailers and the media thought in advance of last Friday. We conveniently forget that we failed to predict it even the day before.

Approaching last Friday, consumers were essentially playing something called the Minority Game. You want to go shopping, but not if there will be huge crowds. If the shops are empty, it is not enjoyable. Like baby bear's porridge, you want it just right, not too many, and not too few.

Parisians leaving the city for their annual month off in August face a similar problem. Giant traffic jams have been experienced at 3 a.m. in the morning, as everyone came to the view that the roads would be quiet at that time. In stock markets, the ideal time to sell is just before the cusp when majority opinion shifts from being bullish to bearish. You are in exactly the right size of minority.

Two Swiss physicists, Damien Challet and Yi-Cheng Zhang, formalised the structure of the game about ten years ago. Since then literally thousands of scientific papers have been written about it. The problem can be stated in words very simply, and it is one with many practical applications. But even using hair-raising maths, it turns out to be fiendishly difficult to solve. In general, there is no strictly rational way to play. To succeed you need to adapt your strategy constantly. The overall outcome is highly uncertain, just like Black Friday.

2 December 2015

Can England win the World Cup?

On a more light-hearted but still serious note, this piece follows from a memorable triumph of the England cricket team over our friends, but also our deadliest foes, from Australia.

The subject is not cricket, however, but soccer. A reason for the unpredictability of many outcomes is that there may be more pure randomness in the world than we like to believe. The outcome of many football games owes more to chance than to differences in skill (Anderson and Sally 2013).

In consequence, even England, it is suggested, could win the World Cup.

As it happens, they were knocked out in the opening sequence of matches in the finals in 2014. But they were only eliminated, for reasons too complicated to explain here, by the 'shock result', as it was invariably called, of the minnows of Costa Rica beating the giants of Italy.

Autumn is fast approaching. The focus of the nation's sporting interest is switching. No sooner have our boys humiliated the Australians, than a new challenge emerges in the shape of two important qualifying games for the soccer World Cup.

The comedian Bob Doolally articulated the views of many when he said: 'If courage, endeavour and guts were what counted, England would be world champions. But as long as football games are decided by arbitrary things like skill, what chance have they got?'

The question is perhaps rather deeper than Mr Doolally suspected. Just how far are games in the World Cup decided by skill, rather than by purely random events?

An obvious example of the latter would be a referee failing to spot that the ball has crossed the goal line. With a different referee, the score would have been awarded. But the outcome of a game may hinge on a myriad of trivial events. A player slips on a divot and misses a crucial tackle, and only a few inches away he would have made it.

One perspective on this is given by the number of goals scored per game in World Cup competitions. A high average suggests that strong teams are beating the weak. Skill shows through. But with a low number per game, random events can easily affect the outcome.

The competition started in 1930. There were only 18 games in the finals, no qualifiers being played, with an average of 3.89 goals per game. Next time, in 1934, there were qualifiers, where 5.35 goals were scored per game. Teams were slightly more equal in the final stages, though the average here was still 4.12. Averages remained high until the finals of 1962: 32 games were played, 89 goals scored, an average of 2.78.

Over the next 50 years, there have been small fluctuations from competition to competition, but the trend is to an even lower number of goals. In 2010, despite an increase in the number of games played to 64, the average was only 2.25 goals a game. With such a low average, and with penalty shoot outs becoming more frequent, it is clear that the differences in skill between the teams in the final stages are pretty low. This even extends to the qualifying stages. In the 2010 competition, there were no fewer than 200 teams, almost every country in the world took part, some of them tiny. But the average number of goals per game was only 2.71.

A new book, *The Numbers Game* by Anderson and Sally, analyses in depth the major national leagues, and in particular the Premier League. Using a mathematical concept known as an 'intransitive triple', a term familiar to economists, they show that the results of almost 50 per cent of games in the Premier League are due to chance rather than skill.

Perhaps it is this very uncertainty of outcome which accounts for the enormous fascination with the game. Even England can win the World Cup.

4 September 2013

References

Anderson, C. and Sally, D. (2013) *The Numbers Game: Why Everything You Know About Football Is Wrong.* London: Penguin.

Arthur, W. B. (1994) *Increasing Returns and Path Dependence in the Economy.* University of Michigan Press.

Arthur, W. B. (1996) Increasing returns and the new world of business. Harvard Business Review, July–August.

Challet, D., Marsili, M. and Zhang, Y.-C. (2005) *Minority Games: Interacting Agents in Financial Markets.* Oxford University Press.

Ormerod, P. (2005) *Why Most Things Fail.* London: Faber and Faber.

Simon, H. A. (1955) A behavioral model of rational choice. *Quarterly Journal of Economics* 69(1): 99–118.

4 INNOVATION

As noted in the Introduction, the market-oriented capitalist economies have one feature which distinguishes them from all other previously and actually existing forms of economic organisation. They generate slow but steady long-run growth.

Two hundred years ago, in the early decades of the nineteenth century, the Industrial Revolution had taken hold in the countries of northwest Europe, and was already beginning to spread elsewhere. The UK at that time was the most developed country in the world. Economic historians argue about the precise figures for real income per head. But even as a conservative estimate, living standards now are 15 to 20 times higher.

The benefits of growth are not confined to higher levels of consumption. Life expectancy has doubled over the past two centuries from the low 40s to the low 80s. Infant mortality has fallen from around 100 per 1,000 births to less than 4. Child labour was prevalent in the industrial factories of the early nineteenth century, and now no one effectively starts work until the age of 18.

The list could go on. But the simple fact is that the slow but persistent underlying growth of capitalist economies has led to a truly dramatic transformation of the world. From a scientific perspective, trying to understand this phenomenon ought to be the main focus of economics. It is by far the most important thing which has happened to the economy.

From the late eighteenth to well into the nineteenth century, it was indeed a major focus of the work of the early economists. For example, Adam Smith's great book of 1776 is entitled *An Inquiry into the Nature and Causes of the Wealth of Nations*.

At a general level, we do know what is required to generate a successful economy. Countries which were poor in the mid-twentieth century and which have copied the general principles of organisation in Western economies and societies have become rich. South Korea is an obvious example. Those which experimented with socialism and planned economies failed.

The scientific question therefore becomes: how can we explain differences in growth rates between countries with the required type of social and economic structure? From a policymakers' perspective, this is a very important thing to know. Even small changes make a huge difference in the long run. A growth rate of 1 per cent a year doubles the size of the economy in 70 years. But a rate of 2 per cent does this in just 35 years.

A single academic paper still dominates the way economists perceive the process of economic growth. This was the model developed in the 1950s by the American Nobel Laureate Robert Solow (1956), which was mentioned in the Introduction.

A key indicator of the importance of a scientific article is how many times it is cited by other scientists in their own work. Very few papers in any discipline have more than 1,000 citations. The one by Solow has nearly 24,000 at a recent count.

To recap from the Introduction, Solow suggested that the output of an economy is determined by three factors: how much labour and how much capital go into the process of production, and something which he called 'technical progress'. We can usefully think of this as innovation in its broadest sense. In other words, not just inventions which advance scientific knowledge, but the dissemination of these inventions in practical applications.

This simple model has provided us with one great empirical insight into the process of growth. Most of the growth which has taken place, certainly in modern times, in the market-oriented economies cannot be explained by increases in the amount of labour and capital which have been used. There has just not been enough of either to account for how much growth has taken place. The implication is that it is mainly due to 'technical progress', or innovation.

This book is not meant to either be a textbook or to provide surveys of the academic economics literature. So it is sufficient to just mention that there has been a lot of work in the 60 years since Solow published his paper. Most of it is devoted to trying to identify the cause of technical progress.

But there has not really been a decisive breakthrough in this area, despite all the efforts which have been made. For example, education in its various forms has often been hypothesised to be a key determinant of technical progress. This raises issues of causality. Do countries become rich because they provide a lot of education, or does the fact that they are rich enable them to afford to provide more education? Certainly, the experience of the UK over the past 25 years does not suggest that a massive expansion in the number of university students is of itself much use in raising the growth rate.

Innovation, then, is the key to understanding the process of economic growth. It is an inherently difficult topic for the discipline of economics. Economics focuses on equilibrium, whereas innovation involves change and disruption.

Innovation need not involve massive scientific breakthroughs like splitting the atom. Indeed, for the most part it takes place in modest ways against an everyday background.

One example will suffice to illustrate the point. On 1 August 1981, MTV, the first 24 hour video music channel was launched on television. The first song it played was iconic, a very catchy, quirky number entitled 'Video Killed the Radio Star'. New technology displaces old. Following on from MTV, almost 40 years ago now, there has been massive innovation in the way in which popular culture is delivered. Facebook, Google, Netflix, YouTube – there is a long list of incredibly successful innovations which impact almost every minute of the day.

The title of the first MTV song echoes the worries of the famous Luddites of the early nineteenth century, traditional workers who were being displaced by tech-nology. They tried to halt the process by smashing the ma-chines which were making them redundant.

Since capitalism first began, this tension has existed. It is easy to see the effects of new technology on particular groups of workers. They lose their jobs. Much less obvious, but ultimately more powerful, is the increase in spending power created for everyone else, as innovation makes the product or service in question cheaper and better.

Whatever happened to all those miners? Shocks and economic resilience

The early 1980s in Britain saw a major dispute between Mrs Thatcher's government and the coal miners' union. This culminated in a bitter strike in 1984–85, which was rapidly followed by the closure of most of what remained of the UK's mines. Even today, there are regular demands for a public enquiry into the clashes which took place between the miners and the police.

This piece was prompted by publicity given to one such call. It looks at the employment experience in the subsequent decades of the local areas in Britain which were dominated by coal mining (Ormerod 2010). This has differed widely. Some have prospered, and registered strong employment growth. Others remain pretty stagnant. But the more militant an area was during the strike, the less well it has done. Changes should be embraced rather than resented.

Where have all the miners gone? To judge by the rhetoric of the BBC and other Leftist media outlets, whole swathes of Britain lie devastated, plagued by rickets, unemployment and endemic poverty – nearly thirty years after the pit closures under Lady Thatcher!

The reality is different. There is indeed a small number of local authority areas where employment has never really recovered from the closures in the 1980s. But, equally, there are former mining areas which have prospered.

Thirty years ago, in 1983, there were 29 local authority areas in the UK, out of a total of over 450, in which mining accounted for more than 10 per cent of total employment. A mere handful of areas still remain scarred by the closures. Wansbeck, on the bleak Northumbrian coast, had 21 per cent of its jobs filled by mining in 1983. Now, employment remains 25 per cent lower than it was then. Elsewhere, reality is not as bad as the image.

The old mining areas at the heads of the South Wales valleys are meant to symbolise industrial decay. But in Merthyr Tydfil, there are 8 per cent more jobs than there were in 1983. Admittedly, in Blaenau Gwent, based on Ebbw Vale, employment is 12 per cent lower. This is hardly permanent devastation. In Easington on the Durham coast, miners made up no less than 41 per cent of all local employment. But even after this devastating blow, losing almost half the area's jobs, employment now is only 9 per cent lower than it was in 1983.

In contrast, there are real success stories. North West Leicestershire and South Staffordshire used to have lots of miners. But employment in both areas is now some 40 per cent – forty! – higher than it was in 1983.

The experience of the individual mining areas differs dramatically in terms of their resilience, their ability to recover economically. Three years ago, I published a short article in *Applied Economics Letters* on the changes in employment in all the mining areas between 1983 and 2002. Total UK employment grew by 23 per cent, and in the ex-mining areas as a whole by just 9 per cent. But it was growth and not decline.

A key influence on this has been the attitude of the workers. Statistical analysis shows that the more militant an area was in the bitter and controversial miners' strike in the winter of 1984–85, the less well it has done subsequently. In Leicestershire, one of the success stories, only 10 per cent ever supported the strike in the first place. In Wansbeck, support was 95 per cent, and even when the strike was ending rapidly in March 1985, 60 per cent were still out.

Economies have the capacity to recover from even the most dramatic adverse shocks, both at national and local levels. But to do this successfully, the workers must be willing to embrace the future rather than cling to the past.

17 April 2013

Economics isn't always the dismal science

Worries are frequently and prominently expressed that innovation is proceeding too rapidly. The Luddites in the early nineteenth century were concerned about a relatively small number of machines in factories. But robots, it is alleged, will proliferate and put huge numbers of people out of work.

This important viewpoint merits the inclusion of two pieces which offer a much more positive view of innovation. The first is based on a very accessible paper published in the leading Journal of Economic Perspectives by the top economic historian Joel Mokyr and his colleagues (Mokyr et al. 2015).

Economics is often described as the dismal science, but it contains cheerful material. A paper by the leading American economic historian Joel Mokyr made for exuberant holiday reading. Written for the top *Journal of Economic*

Perspectives, it is entirely in English and contains not a single mathematical symbol. Mokyr examines the history of anxieties about the economic impact of technology since the late eighteenth century.

We are living through precisely such a phase of worry at present, as fears abound that robots will destroy our jobs and take over the world. There is nothing new under the sun. The same concern was widespread two centuries ago. The machinery installed in new-fangled factories would create mass unemployment.

Mokyr points out neatly that people get anxious at the same time about a problem which has completely opposite implications. Namely, that we are running out of ideas, and the progress of technology will grind to a halt.

The great English economist David Ricardo addressed exactly this question in the early nineteenth century in his *Principles of Political Economy*. Many leading economists in the US share the concern today.

The most famous group objecting to machinery two hundred years ago were the Luddites, who went round smashing it up, along with any unfortunate mill owner they could get their hands on. But the slightly later Captain Swing riots were also widespread, particularly in rural areas, and were often even more dangerous. Mokyr notes that the modern equivalent is the Occupy Wall Street movement, an altogether tamer creature. It turns out that the Swing riots were mainly directed not against the new threshing machines used by farmers, but against the use of cheap immigrant labour from Ireland. Hello?

And in any event, the main complaint made by the working class in the first half of the nineteenth century was about the exceptionally long hours they were required to work, an observation difficult to square with claims that jobs were being eliminated on a large scale.

In the end, the fears of the Luddites that machinery would impoverish workers were not realized, and the main reasons are well understood. Technological change increased the demand for other types of labour that were complementary to the new technologies. So, for example, large numbers of supervisors and managers were needed for the vast new factories and companies. Product innovation created completely new markets which demanded completely new types of job.

The process has continued. As Mokyr says, 'Nineteenth-century political economists lacked an ability to predict new job categories like the personal fashion consultants, cyber security experts, and online-reputation managers of the twenty-first century'.

In fact, the demand for labour has held up far more than was expected. Between 1900 and 1930, for example, weekly hours in American manufacturing fell from 59.6 to 50.6. A simple extrapolation, beloved of doom merchants, would imply only 25.4 hours would be worked by 2015. Of course, innovation is disruptive. But over the 250-year history of capitalism, its positive effects have greatly outweighed the negatives ones of job destruction.

26 August 2015

Could Ernie replace Andy?
The Bank's take on automation

The positive view of the impact of innovation was emphasised in a speech by the Chief Economist of the Bank of England.[1]

The Chief Economist of the Bank of England, Andy Haldane, has been in the news with his predictions that up to 15 million jobs in the UK are at risk of being lost to automation. This is a huge number, around half the total number of people in work today.

Haldane injected a note of humour into his address to the Trades Union Conference, by suggesting that his own job was not at risk. It was unlikely, he said, that an 'Andy robot' would be giving this speech to the TUC even ten years from now. Given the Bank's recent track record in economic forecasting, a cynic might respond in kind. Surely Ernie, the name of the original random number generator used to draw Premium Bonds (the original version of the National Lottery, introduced in the late 1950s), could do just as well.

His speech was far more thoughtful and balanced than the more lurid attention-grabbing points seized on by the media. Haldane pointed out that, since the start of the Industrial Revolution over 250 years ago, there has been a steady and continuous stream of labour-saving advances in technology. It is these which drive productivity, the

---

1   Haldane's speech can be accessed at http://www.bankofengland.co.uk/publications/Documents/speeches/2015/speech864.pdf

amount of output produced per worker. This has risen at an annual average rate of 1.1 per cent since 1750.

In the UK, the employment rate today as a proportion of the total population is around 50 per cent, very similar to levels in the early nineteenth century. The same is true in other countries.

The good news does not end there. The share of wages in the overall economy is very similar to what it was in the eighteenth century. Real wages, living standards, have risen in line with productivity, in complete contradiction to Marx's prediction that capitalism would make workers worse off. And technology has enabled people to work fewer hours and have longer holidays. Compared to a century ago, the average working week has fallen from 50 hours to 30.

The potential problem, according to Haldane, arises through the sheer scale of disruption which might take place. Eventually, automation will benefit society. But it might take a long time for the effects to be absorbed.

Such pessimism may not be justified. The labour market is far more dynamic and evolutionary than most people imagine. The US Bureau for Labor Statistics describes the 'vast amount of job churn' which takes place every single quarter. Millions of companies decide to either expand or contract their workforce on a quarterly basis. Hundreds of thousands of firms open or close from one quarter to the next. Even in recessions, large numbers of jobs are created.

The net changes in employment, the difference between jobs created and jobs lost, in any single quarter are small. But they conceal a vast whirlpool of constant change and flux. The old Soviet Union had 'secure' jobs, but eventually it collapsed. Towns in our regions have a large proportion of the workers employed in 'secure' public sector jobs, but they are poor. Western economies are used to change. It is their life blood and it is what makes them successful.

18 November 2015

Neo-Luddites won't like it, but the UK must keep on (driverless) truckin'

An experiment with driverless trucks on motorways in the UK was announced, provoking the usual outrage and questions about where the new jobs will come from. This piece gives some practical examples in answer to this question.

The announcement that experiments will take place with driverless lorries on UK motorways ought to be a cause for celebration. Once again, human ingenuity is pushing out the frontiers of technology.

But the general reaction in the media has been one of anxiety and concern. Wholly contradictory arguments have been advanced against them.

Driverless cars, it is argued for example, do not mean that you can summon one to your front door and be taken to and from the pub with impunity. The drink-driving laws, the opponents of progress pronounce with confidence, will still apply to the humans being transported. Yet it is also claimed that the concept of responsibility for accidents involving driverless cars does not yet exist. Until it is, they cannot legally be used.

As with the introduction of railways, the law around a revolutionary technology will take some time to evolve. But the idea that a man should walk in front of the train carrying a red flag was soon given short shrift. The new technology was far too convenient to have it impeded in this way.

The opposition to driverless cars and lorries seems almost Luddite in its intensity. People currently employed in and around the activity of driving vehicles will become unemployed. Where will the new jobs come from?

I am writing this in a country house hotel in Aberdeenshire. In the room is a magazine dedicated to weddings. This, a eulogy to expensive popular culture, tells us a great deal about how the labour market evolves.

Many of the activities around modern weddings involve jobs which were either completely non-existent only a few decades ago, or only catered to a tiny number of ultra-rich individuals.

The adverts for venues, for example, usually stress that a dedicated wedding coordinator will be assigned to you during the planning stages. And a dedicated wedding events manager will ensure the day itself goes smoothly. Bridalwear experts can be hired to advise on the choice of costumes. People can, and do, pay substantial fees to be told that 'if you plan to marry at the height of summer in Spain, a heavy material such as velvet is inadvisable'.

Special courses of dance lessons are available so that the bride and groom can perform a 'full-on choreographed, fabulous first dance'. The potential activities around hen and stag events know no bounds. An adventure activity day is offered involving 'Segways or zorbing'.

Specific fitness courses are offered to ensure that not only the bride and groom but their entire supporting cast look suitably 'toned and sculpted'. Even your faithful pooch can be groomed for the occasion, and look glowing through consuming organic dog food. What a pity there was no advert for vegan canine sustenance...

This is a snapshot of how innovation impacts the economy. Technology enables a product or service to be provided more cheaply and at a higher quality. Some people directly involved lose their jobs. But everyone else is made better off, and their extra spending creates entirely new types of jobs.

30 August 2017

Always look on the bright side

In complete contrast to the view that innovation is very rapid and will destroy huge numbers of jobs, there is an influential school of thought, mainly backed by Democrat-supporting American academics, which holds that the pace of innovation has slowed dramatically (King 2014; Gordon 2012). The proponents of this view are just as pessimistic as those who believe that robots will destroy employment. But their worry is that because of a lack of innovation, growth in the future will be much slower than it has been in the past. I cite evidence in support of the view that, if anything, innovation is accelerating.

The American economic recovery carries on apace, with a net rise in employment of almost half a million over the past three months. The Office for National Statistics has decided that the UK never had a double-dip recession, and the texture of the economic news has turned positive.

But economics is not called the dismal science for nothing. What of the longer term? Here, there is no shortage of doom and gloom. Stephen King, chief economist at HSBC, has just published an interesting and well-written book, *When the Money Runs Out*. Pessimism infects the high command of the American academic economics establishment.

The source of these melancholy views is an influential paper by Robert Gordon published by the National Bureau of Economic Research in August 2012. The title poses a stark question: 'Is US economic growth over?' Gordon's answer is basically 'yes'. There are a few nuances to this in his paper, but he takes a bleak view of the prospects for the American economy during the rest of the twenty-first century.

For Gordon, the basic problem is that all the major technological innovations are behind us. The period 1750–1850 saw the steam engine and the railways. In the closing decades of the nineteenth century, the foundations of our modern way of life were laid down with the internal combustion engine and electricity. He argues that in 1960 we entered the information age, and although this has brought benefits, the boost to growth which it provided is now fading.

A key question is whether this is true. Predicting how new technologies will be used is fraught with difficulty, and their full potential can take many decades to realise. The statement made by Thomas Watson, chairman of IBM, in 1943 is notorious: 'I think there is a world market for five computers'.

Even after the event, their impact can be difficult to identify. There is still a powerful school of thought among economic historians that the railway made little difference to the growth of the American economy in the nineteenth century, a proposition which strikes the layperson as absurd but which is nevertheless believed.

But it is not just in the information technology and communications sector where dramatic advances are already taking place. Major breakthroughs in energy use and extractions have been made, with 300 mpg cars, shale gas, and the huge potential of both renewable energy and energy storage. Biotechnology is even more exciting. Humans may soon have the ability to live healthy lives to the age of 200 and beyond. Sociobiology may give us deep new insights into how to deal with major social issues such as drug addiction and crime.

Capitalism has been incredibly inventive during the 250 years of its history, and there is no reason to believe that this will not continue. The crucial requirement is not technological but political. The basic institutional structures of the rule of law and private property must be maintained, so that innovators can reap the fruits of their labours.

3 July 2013

All we are saying: give capitalism a chance

Regardless of one's view of the eventual impact of innovation, there is a marked divergence between the US and the EU

in terms of innovation in recent years (Van Ark et al. 2008).
Since the Brexit referendum, Leave voters have been pillor-
ied in the metropolitan liberal media. 'They were too stupid
to understand the issues involved' is one of the more polite
charges which is made.

But there is a real issue about both the attitude towards
and the ability to innovate of many of the countries of the EU.

Is there a secret Leninist cell operating at a high level in
the European Commission's headquarters in Brussels?
One which is dedicated to the overthrow of the capitalist
structures of the European Union?

The evidence from this past week is certainly consist-
ent with this hypothesis. The demand for an additional
£1.7 billion payment from the UK is based on calculations
backdated to 1995. Revisions to the way in which GDP is
constructed means that Britain is better off than was
previously thought, so we have to pay more. A pure gift to
anti-EU political parties.

The saga does not end there. If the UK's success is to be
punished, it is perhaps logical, in this twisted view of the
world, to reward the failing French economy with a rebate.
But Germany, too, is due a repayment. Incredibly, Cyprus
and Greece, catastrophic basket cases, have to pay more.

The fundamental problem with the EU is that the basic
virtues of a successful capitalist economy are being re-
pressed more systematically across the board. There is a
strong consensus among economists, based on firm evidence, that the main determinant of long-term growth in
developed economies is innovation.

The European Commission pays a great deal of lip service to this, but Europe in general still lags considerably behind America in terms of innovation. The concept covers a range of factors. One is learning how to produce more of the same kind of output from a given set of inputs, which is an ongoing process throughout the economy.

Much more importantly, inventions create the possibility of developing entirely new kinds of output, whether goods or services. Inventions are necessary for growth, but even more important is the ability of an economy to turn inventions from being ideas which enable the creation of new products, to the actual creation of the products themselves.

The massive companies created in the information and communications technology sector (ICT) in recent decades have almost all been American. And to the list which includes Microsoft, Google and Facebook can now be added Alibaba, the new ICT giant from China.

An important article by Bart van Ark and colleagues in the top-ranked *Journal of Economic Perspectives* in 2008 examined the widening productivity gap between Europe and the US in the two decades immediately prior to the financial crash. Their conclusion was unequivocal: 'the European productivity slowdown is attributable to the slower emergence of the knowledge economy in Europe compared to the United States'.

This lack of dynamism shows itself in the shorter-term inability of many European economies to recover from the crisis. Of course, a key reason for this has been the macro-economic and financial policies of the Commission and the European Central Bank. But the EU has increasingly become an area in which it is much easier to make money by what economists call rent-seeking than by innovation. Exploiting a monopoly, lobbying the regulator, ticking some boxes, these are what pay. Innovations are disruptive, but Europe needs to encourage them more than ever.

29 October 2014

Artificial Intelligence and the future

The sharp contrast between America and Europe is also the focus of this piece, which looks specifically at the rapidly advancing science of artificial intelligence (Aletras et al. 2016; Crawford and Calo 2016; Executive Office of the President 2016).

The rise of artificial intelligence (AI) continues to generate concerns. The latest furore emerged at the start of this week. Researchers in the top-ranked University College London computer science department claimed that an AI algorithm correctly predicts the outcome of 79 per cent of cases heard at the European Court of Human Rights.

The current fear of AI, certainly among the arts graduates who write the editorials in the national quality press, is such that the study was firmly denounced. Computers can never replace human knowledge and experience in these matters.

But in real life, algorithms are being used increasingly by law firms. The law is essentially a series of rules which have been developed over time. Many areas of civil law are enormously complex. Computers can sift through huge amounts of material and save a great deal of expensive human time.

The use of AI is proliferating rapidly in many diverse areas, from the early identification of diseases, to the reduction of energy costs for data centres and to the decision on whether or not to grant a loan. An article in the latest issue of the august scientific journal *Nature* by Kate Crawford and Ryan Calo shows that investment in technologies that use AI in the US has soared from some $400 million in 2011 to well over $2 billion last year. They quote IBM's chief executive, Ginni Rometty, saying that she sees a $2 *trillion* opportunity in AI systems over the next decade.

Earlier this month, the White House published its report on the future of AI, based on four workshops with leading specialists held across America on how AI will change the way we live.

The American government recognises that this highly disruptive new technology creates new risks in many ways. But so, too, did the railways. During the opening ceremony of the Liverpool to Manchester line in 1830, the engine *Rocket* hit and killed a cabinet minister, William Huskisson. Serious suggestions were made that men with red flags should walk in front of trains, which would have defeated the whole point of the technology.

But these risks did not stop railways from spreading across the world. In the same way, the White House report concludes that 'AI holds the potential to be a major driver of economic growth and social progress'.

The report is packed full with both interesting information and perspectives on AI. It is also a case study in why the US continues to be by far the most innovative economy in the world. By and large, the Americans leave innovation to commercial companies. But where the national interest is concerned, the public sector works in symbiosis with the private. They plan a huge programme of basic research in AI, but with a firm eye to its practical application.

Just as the US did with biotech, the aim is to develop a critical mass of money, skills and ideas funded by the government, which companies then build on. America is once again embracing the future.

26 October 2016

Biotech contradicts accusation of City short-termism

In liberal elite circles, the US and the UK financial markets are often criticised for being too short term, in contrast to the supposedly longer-term view taken in Continental Europe.

A book by Geoffrey Owen, former editor of the Financial Times, and Sussex academic Michael Hopkins on the highly innovative biotech industry – Science, the State and the City – contradicts this view strongly (Owens and Hopkins 2016).

Biotech inventions take at least 10 years to be developed, tested and brought to market, and 15 years is more the norm. But America and Britain, in complete contrast to their allegedly short-term outlook, lead the world in biotech. The Owen and Hopkins book also describes not only how successful industries evolve, but how attempts to develop them by diktat and a top-down approach have proved far less successful.

The proposed takeover of the hugely successful ARM Holdings by the Japanese giant, Softbank is in the news. ARM is well placed to exploit the white-hot concept of the internet of things.

The UK has also performed well in biotechnology. But the industry came under scrutiny last week at a Centre for the Study of Financial Innovation seminar. Geoffrey Owen, former editor of the *Financial Times*, and Sussex academic Michael Hopkins introduced their new book, *Science, the State and the City*.

On a world scale, the UK is second only to the US in biotech, outstripping everyone else in key performance indicators for the industry. Owen and Smith's book is prompted by the fact that we are a very long way behind the leader. For example, US scientists have 45 per cent of all the citations in life sciences in academic journals, and we have 15 per cent. The UK government spends roughly double the amount in health research and development of our European neighbours, but America spends at least 10 times as much as we do.

Our distant second places, in these and other areas which determine the success of a high technology industry, feedback on each other and cumulate. As a result, the market capitalisation of US biotech firms is more than 20 times as big as those of the UK.

Why has this happened? After all, what is possibly the greatest scientific discovery of the twentieth century and which made all this possible – the double helix structure of DNA – was by scientists based in Britain, Crick and Watson.

Owen and Hopkins carefully dismantle the myth that it is the short-term outlook of the City which is responsible. This is often compared unfavourably to the long-termist approach of Germany and Japan. But it is exactly the allegedly short-term Anglo-Saxon economies which are by far the best performers in biotech, an industry in which the time period from scientific discovery to marketable product is at least 10 and often as much as 15 years.

They do note, however, that British academics appear more interested in publishing academic papers and securing yet more research grants than in the process of commercialisation. There is a steady flow of entrepreneurial scientists who found biotech companies, but it is very much a minority taste in the UK compared to America.

The US industry clusters, with firms concentrated in San Francisco and Boston. So does the British, mainly near Cambridge. But attempts by European governments to develop clusters in a top-down dirigiste way have not worked.

Owen and Hopkins argue that American success is based on a bottom-up, evolutionary process, in which a successful ecosystem emerges rather than being designed. Entrepreneurial academics, teaching hospitals and venture capital spontaneously collaborated for mutual benefit. The US government also helped, with its massive funding for research and regulatory changes which helped the industry. The lesson is a general one for development. The public sector can facilitate but not command success. That arises from the drive of individuals with proper incentives.

27 July 2016

Stranded assets and innovation

Energy is another sector where innovation is crucial. There are genuine concerns about global warming. Western politicians have tried to address this through changing the incentives to consume energy such as carbon pricing, or by rules and regulations. These approaches run up against the basic problem that people around the world still want to get better off. They want economic growth, and so there are limits as to how far approaches which restrict the consumption of energy can go.

This piece offers a different view. The Governor of the Bank of England had made a speech warning that companies with large carbon assets risked them being 'stranded' (Carney 2015). They appear to have value now, but they would be increasingly unable to extract them in the future because of restrictions on their use.

More or less at the same time, and by coincidence, a paper from the Breakthrough Institute in California argued that it is technology – innovation – which disrupts and alters the patterns of energy consumption (Schellenberger and Nordhaus 2015). It is innovation which will help solve our problems in this area.

The Governor of the Bank of England, Mark Carney, courted the wrath of the fossil fuel industry in a speech at the end of last month. He argued that investors in the sector face 'potentially huge losses'. Actions by governments to try to head off climate change could make most reserves of coal, oil and gas 'literally unburnable'.

Tougher rules and regulations on the use of carbon-based energy, along with higher taxes, could leave the assets of fossil fuel companies 'stranded'. 'Stranded' is the new buzz word in climate change circles. Assets may be left stranded in the ground because it is no longer practical to extract them at any meaningful rate.

A fascinating and closely argued paper by Ted Nordhaus and Michael Shellenberger of the California-based Breakthrough Institute puts a different perspective on how energy assets become stranded. They give plenty of historical examples.

In the middle of the nineteenth century, Americans used 13 million gallons of whale oil each year, mainly to light their lamps. Within two years of the first oil strike in 1858, the petroleum industry achieved that level. Whalers quit their jobs to work in the oil fields. The asset of whale oil was left 'stranded' in the whales in the ocean. From the first stirrings of industry in England several hundred years ago to well into the nineteenth century, wood was the primary source of energy for our factories and blast furnaces. Coal stranded the wood fuel industry. In 1900, just 2–3 per cent of England was covered by forests. Today, 10–12 per cent is.

Nordhaus and Shellenberger argue that large-scale asset stranding in the global energy context will remain, as it has always been, primarily driven by technological change. Whether from wood to coal in the nineteenth century or, as is currently underway in the US, from coal to gas in the twenty-first, the primary driver of wholesale transitions to new sources of energy has been the fact that the new source of energy was cleaner, cheaper and more useful.

This is the classic concept of a disruptive technology put forward by the great Harvard economist Joseph Schumpeter. Such technologies are so superior they simply sweep aside competition. Within a few years of the coming of the railways, the prestige London to Edinburgh stagecoach service disappeared.

Humanity's quest for more heat, light and power has been the main driver of invention and innovation. Only this month, Bill Gates announced a project to work with the Chinese government to develop a next-generation nuclear reactor that not only cannot melt down but also recycles waste as fuel.

The demand for energy, especially in the developing world and countries like India and China with their massive, aspirant populations, will continue to grow. Carbon pricing, emissions caps, the whole paraphernalia of regulation which Western countries might bring in, will not alter this demand. Fossil fuels may indeed become stranded. This will happen not because of bureaucrats, but because of innovation and breakthroughs in nuclear and alternative energy technologies.

21 October 2015

Britain's New Industrial Policy: can we learn from the mistakes of the past?

This was inspired by a book by Bill Janeway, who led the Warburg Pincus Investment team (Janeway 2012). A fundamental point which he makes is that both scientific research and invention, and its subsequent exploitation through practical innovations, necessarily involves a great deal of waste. Many such innovative ventures will fail. They cannot provide the security of projects which marginally increase knowledge, or make trivial improvements to existing technology (Department for Business, Innovation and Skills 2013).

The phrase 'industrial policy' seems to take us decades back in time. In 1964, a powerful catchphrase of the new Labour Prime Minister, Harold Wilson, was the need for Britain to embrace the 'white heat of the technological revolution'. Sadly, by the 1970s this vision had deteriorated into a list of institutions, stuffed with dull businessmen and trade unionists, meeting to decide how to prop up yet another failed sector of the UK economy.

But the concept is now back in vogue. Perhaps surprisingly, given the historical experience, the coalition chose to preserve Labour's Technology Strategy Board (TSB) quango. The TSB has a budget of £400 million to 'accelerate UK economic growth by stimulating and supporting business-led innovation'. A key way in which it plans to do this is through the purchasing decisions of the public sector.

In October, Sir Andrew Whitty, CEO of GlaxoSmith-Klein, produced a report commissioned by the Department for Business, Innovation and Skills on how universities can better support economic growth and drive exports.

Whitty calls for the creation of 'Arrow Projects', supporting cutting-edge technologies and inventions where the UK leads the world, with, in an excruciating pun, 'universities at the tip'. Universities and Science minister David Willets eulogised the report. In language redolent of Soviet

Five Year Plans, he stated that 'we are making strides to help commercialise the work of universities under the Eight Great Technologies'.

It is easy to mock both the symbolism and the content of speeches and reports such as this. But the intention deserves to be taken very seriously. Thinking back again to the decades of the 60s and 70s, far-left radicals used to denounce the 'military-industrial complex' of the US. Yet it has been precisely the interplay between the defence and security sectors and high-tech commercial companies that has led to America continuing to lead the world in technological innovations.

A fascinating new book by Bill Janeway, *Doing Capitalism in the Innovation Economy*, gives many such examples. The creation of the internet is well known, others include automatic speech recognition and digital computing. Janeway has made a personal fortune, not by financial speculation or by trading complex derivatives, but by developing and leading the Warburg Pincus Investment team which provided financial backing to a whole series of companies which built the internet economy.

A fundamental point which he makes is that both scientific research and invention, and its subsequent exploitation through practical innovations, necessarily involves a great deal of waste.

This is something which British bureaucrats have, in the past, been unable to grasp. Ideas which are genuinely path-breaking cannot be conceived in advance.

And, equally, the value of their practical applications is something which cannot be imagined before it happens.

This means that many such ventures will fail. They cannot provide the box-ticking security of projects which add tiny amounts of knowledge, or which make trivial improvements to an existing technology. So, Arrow and the TSB are to be welcomed, provided that they, and the Public Accounts Committee, recognise that most things fail.

4 December 2013

Why cricket is like spam

This takes a more light-hearted but still serious view about the process of evolution in human affairs. The England cricket team had just failed abysmally in their second innings to reach a massive total set by Australia. But the ability of teams to make big scores in such situations does seem to have improved dramatically in recent years.

The piece takes a longer-term perspective on the evolutionary struggle between bat and ball in cricket. A close parallel exists in the world of email spam, where the spammers and the defenders also play an innovative, evolutionary game (Colbaugh and Glass 2013).

The holiday season gets into full swing, but a shadow has been cast by the abysmal failure of our boys to get anywhere near the enormous target of 509 which Australia set them to win in the second Test match. It may seem preposterous even to have thought they would. But a revolution seems to be taking place in the ability of teams to make large scores in the fourth innings.

S. Rajesh, the stats editor of the website ESPNcricinfo, has a fascinating piece on whether batting in the last innings has become easier. In the 140-year history of Test cricket, teams have scored 350 or more in the final innings on only 49 occasions. Of these, no fewer than 21 have been in the past 10 years. The chances of winning when faced with such a challenge still remain low. Only four sides won in the most recent decade, and only nine in total, but the ability to score heavily seems to have leapt up.

Before World War II, teams made 350 or more just five times. Admittedly, one of these was the monumental 654–6 which England made in South Africa in 1939. The match was timeless, with England being set 696 to win. But at the end of the tenth day, the match had to be abandoned as a draw so that the team could catch their ship home. In the five decades from 1945 to 1995, with many more Tests being played, 350 was exceeded only 14 times.

Rajesh offers some explanations for the dramatic rise in large fourth innings totals. Higher scoring rates, boosted by the techniques of Twenty20 cricket, mean that teams tend to start their final innings earlier in the match, when the pitch has had less chance to deteriorate. And in general pitch maintenance is better, so they crumble less.

This all sounds plausible and rational. But the change may not be a permanent one. The world of spam filtering illustrates why. The attacking side, the spammers, constantly change their strategies to try and break through, and the defenders also develop their techniques. At the moment, they are on top, with the US company Symantec claiming that spam rates are now lower than ever.

But we have been here before. In 2012, the infamous Russian botnet, Grum, was taken down by spam fighters, and spam fell by a half, only to bounce back. In the same way, there are two sides in a cricket match, and strategies evolve over time. They just take longer to work out and perfect.

In the inter-war period, massive scores were made very rapidly, as improvements in batting techniques dominated. The fielding side then gained the upper hand. Fielders became more athletic and defensive placements got better. Bowling techniques evolved in their ability to contain the batsman.

In any evolutionary system in which two adversaries face each other, fluctuations in outcomes will take place. Spam and cricket are just two examples. Maybe even England will be able to learn how to score more than 103.

22 July 2015

References

Aletras, N., Tsarpatsanis, D., Preotiuc-Pietro, D. and Lampos, V. (2016) Predicting judicial decisions of the European Court of Human Rights: a natural language processing perspective. *PeerJ Computer Science* 2: e93 (https://doi.org/10.7717/peerj -cs.93).

Carney, M. (2015) Breaking the tragedy of the horizon – climate change and financial stability (http://www.bankofengland.co .uk/publications/Documents/speeches/2015/speech844.pdf).

Colbaugh, R. and Glass, K. (2013) Moving target defense for adaptive adversaries (https://www.osti.gov/scitech/servlets/purl/ 1115999).

Crawford, K. and Calo, R. (2016) There is a blind spot in AI research. *Nature* 538: 311–13 (doi:10.1038/538311a).

Department for Business, Innovation and Skills (2013) Encouraging a British invention revolution: Sir Andrew Witty's review of universities and growth.

Executive Office of the President (2016) Artificial intelligence, automation and the economy, December (https://www.white house.gov/sites/whitehouse.gov/files/images/EMBARGOED %20AI%20Economy%20Report.pdf).

Gordon, R. J. (2012) Is US economic growth over? Faltering innovation confronts the six headwinds. NBER Working Paper 18315.

Janeway, B. (2012) *Doing Capitalism in the Innovation Economy.* Cambridge University Press.

King, S. D. (2014) *When the Money Runs Out: The End of Western Affluence.* Yale University Press.

Mokyr, J., Vickers, C. and Ziebarth, N. L. (2015) The history of technological anxiety and the future of economic growth: is this time different? *Journal of Economic Perspectives* 29(3): 31–50.

Ormerod, P. (2010) Resilience after local economic shocks. *Applied Economics Letters* 17(5): 503–7.

Owens, G. and Hopkins, M. (2016) *Science, the State and the City.* Oxford University Press.

Schellenberger, M. and Nordhaus, T. (2015) How to strand assets: nature saving through disruptive technological change (https://thebreakthrough.org/index.php/voices/michael -shellenberger-and-ted-nordhaus/how-to-strand-assets).

Solow, R. M (1956) A contribution to the theory of economic growth. *Quarterly Journal of Economics* 70(1): 65–94.

Van Ark, B., O'Mahoney, M. and Timmer, M. P. (2008) The productivity gap between Europe and the United States: trends and causes. *Journal of Economic Perspectives* 22(1): 25–44.

5   NETWORKS

One theme running throughout this book is that scientific theories are approximations to reality. They make assumptions which simplify the massive complexity of the world, in order to try and understand it.

Another theme is that economics is fundamentally a theory about how agents choose between alternatives.

In economic theory, agents are connected and their decisions can be affected by the choices made by others. But the influence is subtle. The connections and the influence are *in*direct, via the consequences for prices of the decisions to buy and sell which others make. If the demand for something I like goes up, and the producers raise their prices as a result, I am affected.

But I am still assumed to like exactly the same things as before the price went up. It is just that I might not be able to afford to buy as much as I would have done before. The decisions of other people affect me, but only in this indirect way.

How reasonable is it to assume that individuals operate autonomously, isolated from the direct influences of others, in terms of what they like and what they don't – their tastes and preferences, as economists say?

Throughout history, we can observe examples of human behaviour which clearly violate this assumption. We sometimes copy the behaviours, choices, opinions of others. In other words, we follow the choices made by others.

We can see it in the fashions in pottery which anthropologists have documented in the Middle Eastern Hittite Empire of three and a half millennia ago. And we can see it today in the behaviour of traders on financial markets, where the propensity to follow the herd can lead all too easily to the booms and crashes we have experienced.

Scientists such as Robin Dunbar have argued that our anomalously large brain (compared to other mammals) evolved precisely because, from an evolutionary perspective, copying – observing and then doing what someone else on your network is doing – is often a very successful strategy to follow.

Economists are of course aware of markets in which fashion drives behaviour. They are aware of what they refer to as 'herding behaviour' in financial markets. But in the textbooks, these, if they are mentioned at all, are seen as rather unusual.

Special tools have to be pulled out of the box in order to understand them. For the most part, the standard model in the box is still the one to use – the one that assumes that my preferences are independent of yours, and vice versa.

But in an increasing number of contexts, the choices people make, their attitudes, their opinions, are influenced directly by other people. The medium via which this influence spreads is the social network.

Often, social networks are thought of as purely a web-based phenomenon: sites such as Facebook. These can indeed influence behaviour. But it is real-life social networks – family, friends, colleagues – that can also be important in helping us shape our preferences and beliefs, what we like and what we do not like.

It is in cyber society, above all, where the assumption that a person's preferences are independent of those of others is not really tenable. By definition, we are highly connected on networks in cyber society, and these networks influence our behaviour directly.

So, for example, when we use a search engine, we will typically be presented with a large, often an extremely large, number of potential sites to visit. A key determinant of the order in which they appear on the screen is the numbers of other people who have selected the sites when searching for the same thing. The more people who clicked on a site previously, the more likely it is to appear at the top of the list.

We will never know who these people are. But we are connected to them on a network. Their choices will almost certainly affect our choice of which sites we click on. Many people rarely go beyond the first page of alternatives which comes up on the screen.

In the section above on uncertainty and the limits to knowledge, we looked at a different aspect of the assumptions which economics makes. This concerned the ability of agents to gather and process the information which is available about the choices they face in any given context. It is cyber society there, as well, which creates problems for the conventional theory of choice in economics.

These two assumptions – independence of preferences and the ability to process information – are linked in the work of one of the greatest social scientists of the second half of the twentieth century, Herbert Simon. We met him in the piece of 20 November 2013 on the World Chess Championship.

In 1955, Simon published a paper in the *Quarterly Journal of Economics* with the seemingly innocuous title of 'A behavioural model of rational choice'. But it proved to be enormously influential. It was the inspiration for both experimental and behavioural economics, two of the fastest growing areas of economics in the past 30 years. It should be said that, although it is by no means as mathematical as most modern articles in economic journals, it is not at all an easy read.

One of the hallmarks of a genius is that his or her work is often years, and sometimes decades, ahead of its time. This is certainly the case with Simon's 1955 paper.

Economics, whether mainstream or behavioural, has still not absorbed its central message. Even in the world of the 1950s, Simon believed that humans were bombarded with so much information that we often lacked the ability to process it. The economic theory of rational choice was a non-starter in many situations. Its assumptions were simply not reasonable approximations to reality. We could only cope with a tiny fraction of much of the information which is available.

His style is somewhat dated now, but a key sentence from his article reads: 'the task is to replace the global rationality of economic man with a kind of rational behavior which is compatible with the access to information and computational capacities that are actually possessed by organisms, including man, in the kinds of environments in which such organisms exist'.

Simon believed strongly that the model of rational economic individuals could not be modified to deal with this problem. It had to be 'replaced'. He argued that when making decisions, agents used rules of thumb, or 'heuristics' in the economic jargon. These are simple rules which cut through the complications of rational choice theory.

An important example of such a rule, he believed, is to copy the decisions of others. The sites people click on after an internet search is a practical example of the concept.

But how do we make this rule useful in practice? Standard economic theory has the advantage that it is well understood, and is claimed to be useful in almost every single context, regardless of time or place. Even if we do not subscribe to every single one of its assumptions, its central insight, that agents react to incentives, is supported very strongly indeed by empirical evidence in many contexts.

The last twenty years or so have seen two important scientific developments, outside of economics, which greatly enhance our understanding of behaviour on the internet and social media.

The first is the development of the mathematics of networks. How ideas or behaviour spread can be very sensitive to the particular structure of the network. For example, is there a small number people or sites to which large numbers of others are connected in a given context, or do most people and sites have roughly the same number of connections?

The second is even more recent. This is the development of AI and machine learning algorithms in computer science. These enable us, for example, to obtain a complete map of the structure of a network in cyber space, rather than having to rely on approximations to a known theoretical structure.

Machine learning can be used to measure the level of positive or negative sentiment on a network. This might put in reach the ability, for the first time ever, to begin to quantify Keynes's concept of 'animal spirits', discussed in the Introduction and which he believed was the main reason for the booms and recessions which take place.

Both the maths of networks and machine learning algorithms are at the forefront of science, and the fields are developing and evolving rapidly. In my opinion, combining these with the insights of economics offers the opportunity to obtain a much better practical understanding of how the economy works.

This might seem scientific utopianism. The more cynical can certainly point to examples in the past where the promise of major breakthroughs in, say, artificial intelligence, was not borne out in practice. But in my view, building alliances with mathematicians and computer scientists is the way to really push economics forward.

Thomas Schelling, polymath of genius

Thomas Schelling not only received the Nobel Prize in economics, but was a great polymath. One of his contributions was to develop a behavioural rule based on the principle of copying which is relevant in a wide range of practical situations.

As a social scientist, he found inspiration in the most mundane events. His major scientific work in this area was inspired by an article in the sports pages of his local newspaper in Chicago (Schelling 1973).

He died at the end of 2016, and the piece is a tribute to his work (Schelling 1971, 2005). It describes his network-based copying theory of decision making, which has been applied in contexts such as smoking, binge drinking and crime.

An appealing aspect of Schelling's model, to some economists at least, is that while it is based on networks and on preferences which are decidedly not independent, it invokes an important concept in economics. This is the idea of 'externalities'. A polluting vehicle, for example, imposes costs on other people which are external to the costs incurred by the owner as he or she drives along.

Schelling, very neatly, interpreted copying behaviour as an example of an externality. The more people on my social network who, for example, stop smoking, the more the pressures are on me also to stop. Their personal decisions to stop have potential consequences for how other people might behave. In short, they generate externalities.

Last year was a year of celebrity deaths. But perhaps the most significant of all received very little coverage. Just before Christmas, Thomas Schelling, Nobel Laureate in economics, died aged 95.

In the early, tense years of the Cold War between America and the Soviet Union in the late 1940s and 1950s,

Schelling's ideas were enormously influential in preventing nuclear conflict from breaking out. As he pointed out in his Nobel Prize lecture, there was a real danger of this.

The US government invested heavily in the then new science of game theory. How do you handle a weapon which is so devastating you do not want to use it, while at the same time you must convince the other side that you might? Schelling was instrumental in creating the strategy of credible threats.

But his mind ranged powerfully over a wide range of disparate issues. Our understanding of crime, obesity, smoking, binge drinking – a whole host of social problems – has been improved substantially by Schelling's work. He saw that there are underlying similarities in how they develop.

His most important work in this area was published in 1973, in a paper with the fantastic title 'Hockey helmets, concealed weapons and daylight saving'. Schelling's inspiration was a piece in the sports section of a newspaper about ice hockey, a game even more brutal than Rugby League.

A star player had suffered serious head injuries from the flying puck while not wearing a helmet. The reporter interviewed other leading players, none of whom wore helmets. It was clear that they understood the very real dangers involved. A rational economic person, weighing up the costs and benefits, would always wear a helmet. But when asked why not, a top boy answered, 'I don't because the other guys don't'.

Schelling crystallised this into a mathematical concept he called 'binary choice with externalities'. The choice facing an individual is binary. Either you wear a helmet or you don't. Either you smoke, or you don't. But your choice may affect how other people in your peer group make their choices. If no one else wears a helmet, you look soft by wearing one. If all your friends smoke, you may do so just to fit in. So the decision of an individual can have effects which are 'external' to the decision itself. Understanding this is crucial to policymakers trying to influence the outcome. Rational choice theory may not always apply.

His ideas on game theory live on. Indeed, they appear to influence President-elect Trump. Trump sent out many signs that he wants to work with Putin's Russia. But just before Christmas, he tweeted, inexplicably to many, that America should expand its nuclear arsenal. He was in fact making a credible threat. Putin, an ex-KGB man, knew that it was Reagan ratcheting up defence spending which finally broke the old Soviet Union. So Trump signals in a single tweet: we want to cooperate, but if you don't, your economy will collapse as you try to keep up with us.

Thomas Schelling, polymath of genius, I salute you!

4 January 2017

A stitch in time. We need smarter government, but less of it

Over four years previously, readers had been introduced briefly to Thomas Schelling. The then Mayor of London, the flamboyant Boris Johnson, had just made a speech to the CBI in which he had attacked corporate tax avoidance and excessive executive pay. The more these were deemed to be acceptable in the relevant social groups, the more likely these would not just persist but increase.

Almost at the same time, two economists published a highly technical, detailed analysis of cheating in exams in a top journal (Lucifora and Tonello 2015). They found that the more people do it, the more likely it is that yet more will follow their example. The effects feedback on each other, and a small snowball can turn into an avalanche.

Policymakers have not yet learned how to cope satisfactorily with a world in which these behavioural feedbacks have become commonplace. Once the process has started, it becomes hard to stop as the externalities kick in. But if a successful early-stage intervention could be made, these cascades of behaviour could be halted in their tracks. We need smarter government, not necessarily more government.

What is the connection between the content of Boris Johnson's speech this week to the CBI, tax avoidance and evasion, executive pay, petty crime and plagiarism by students? This is yet another one where economics can help us with the solution. Economists have long used the example of a factory which imposes costs on other people in the neighbourhood through the pollution it generates. They refer to such costs as 'externalities'. These are costs external to the factory itself.

Thomas Schelling, a Nobel prizewinner like blockbuster author Daniel Kahneman, extended the concept to the social domain 40 years ago in his enigmatic paper, 'Hockey helmets, concealed weapons and daylight saving time: binary choice with externalities'. The idea here is that the eventual impact of a social choice by an individual can be magnified manyfold. The behaviour, whether it is good or bad, may be copied by his or her peers, and so generates social externalities.

Two Italian economists, Claudio Lucifora and Marco Tonello at Milan, have just published a detailed study, replete with heavy-duty maths, on cheating in exams, something which is now widespread in many European countries, including the UK. They find, perhaps not surprisingly, that the more people do it, the more likely it is that yet more will follow their example. The effects feedback on each other, and a small snowball can turn into an avalanche.

The authors trace the origins of the current wave of plagiarism and cheating right back to the school classroom, to things which by themselves seem pretty innocuous, such as teachers tolerating minor instances of homework copying. The same thing takes place with the 'broken window' effect on petty crime. Most crime takes place in poor neighbourhoods, which tend to be a bit run down. But rigorous enforcement of standards, such as mending broken windows quickly, can have a big impact not just on the ambience but on the values of a local estate.

The executive pay boom began back in the 1980s, with a few examples such as the hapless Cedric Brown, chief executive of the newly privatised British Gas, who increased his pay to the then outrageous level of £400,000 a year. Despite public opprobrium, he got away with it and other executives saw that he had. The Mayor called for companies to show more socially responsible behaviour. But we are by now a very long way down the track where virtually the only focus of the corporate ethos is to maximise shareholder value and executive rewards.

Once the genie is out of the bottle, it is very difficult to put back in. The instinct of government is to want to do more, to spend more money, to regulate more. We don't need more government. We need smarter government, using the waves of information on the web and modern tools of analysis to identify potentially harmful trends at an early stage. Fixing the broken window does not need armies of bureaucrats. It just needs to be done early enough.

21 November 2012

Echo chamber of garbage

One aspect of the networked, modern world which appears to panic policymakers is the storms which gather very rapidly on social media. Once a theme takes hold, it can spread like wildfire. Trial by Twitter is becoming commonplace, with the focus of hostility having to perform penance for his or her crimes, real or imagined.

The Greater Manchester Police were put in the stocks in May 2016. They carried out a simulated terrorist attack on a major retail outlet, in which the attackers represented themselves as jihadists. Despite the close connection of this aspect of the exercise to the real world, there was a storm of abuse, and the police grovelled.

The piece focuses on a very mathematical analysis by a team of leading scientists of Twitter (Del Vicario et al. 2015). They conclude that users frequently form communities of interest which foster confirmation bias, segregation and polarisation. This has worrying consequences.

Greater Manchester Police staged a simulated terror attack in the massive Trafford Park retail complex last week. As with many real-life atrocities, the carnage began with the cry 'Allahu Akbar!' Following a storm of protest on Twitter, the police felt forced to apologise.

Almost at the same time, a frenzied chorus rose up demanding the resignation of the BBC's political editor, Laura Kuenssberg, for having had the temerity to suggest that the local election results were something less than a complete triumph for the Great Leader and Teacher, Jezza. This campaign was halted by the extremely sexist nature of many of the comments posted by left-wing Twitterati.

The way the Kuenssberg saga ended is in fact very unusual. Following a storm of outrage on social media about a statement or an action, the 'guilty' party almost invariably confesses his or her crime and issues a heartfelt apology to the raving crowd.

Social media is a new and radically disruptive technology. It is hardly surprising that traditional institutions and social norms have not yet adapted to the challenges which are raised. Many thousands of voices were raised against the police for their allegedly racist opening cry, with virtually no one springing to their defence. It seemed that public opinion was firmly against them, and so they bowed to pressure and apologised.

But Twitter, along with other social media outlets, is in many circumstances simply an echo chamber. When the polling booths in the Scottish referendum closed in 2014, many in the SNP leadership were convinced they had won. Their researchers had carried out seemingly sophisticated analysis of social media, and concluded the 'Yes' campaign was ahead. The actual result gave rise in turn to all sorts of conspiracy theories, bouncing backwards and forwards between diehard pro-independence Scots.

Late last summer, the US Army carried out a routine training exercise called Jade Helm 15. This sparked a torrent of concerns on social media, a prominent one being that the federal government was planning to invade Texas and civil war was imminent.

A team of top statistical physicists published a paper in January this year in the prestigious *Proceedings of the National Academy of Science*. They find that the problems are widespread in social media, with users frequently forming communities of interest which foster confirmation bias, segregation and polarisation. Biased narratives fomented by unsubstantiated rumours, mistrust and paranoia proliferate.

How do we know whether to take a trend on social media seriously, or whether to just dismiss it as a bunch of fruitcakes egging each other on? A topic which has only a small number of mentions in each of several different social media communities is potentially far more significant than one which has a huge number in just one. Public bodies need to learn how to differentiate between social media topics, and not just routinely capitulate to the mob.

18 May 2016

Alas, poor Cecil! Economic theory and the death of a lion

A major problem for policymakers in our highly connected cyber society is that what we might describe as the objective content of a story may have little or no connection with whether it spreads across social media or not. Rational policymakers may believe something is important. Social media may decide otherwise.

The piece of was inspired by the story of Cecil the lion. Cecil was a feline patriarch patrolling the plains of Zimbabwe. He was shot, perfectly legally it appears, by a big game hunter. Zimbabwe has a kleptocratic, hugely incompetent and murderous government. But none of these important themes were mentioned in the Twitter storm. Indeed, the Mugabe government was virtually eulogised, as demands were made to forcibly send the unfortunate American hunter to Zimbabwe to be executed.

The effective regulation of hunting rare species raises difficult questions for economics, and the work of Nobel Laureate Elinor Ostrom is particularly illuminating (Ostrom 2009).

Alas, poor Cecil! Close personal friend of mine, sadly dead now. The catch phrases of the Scottish comedian Bob Doolally capture the outpourings of grief among the Twitterati at the death of the now famous lion.

The mourning is mixed with incoherent rage, as long-standing opponents of torture and capital punishment demand that the dentist have his teeth pulled out without anaesthetic and then be sent to Zimbabwe to be hanged.

Yet the story illustrates two deep features of the current world. We can usefully reflect on the truly appalling outrages which have been inflicted on Zimbabwe by President Mugabe. At the start of his regime, he used Cuban and North Korean troops to murder 20,000 political opponents. One of the most fertile countries in Africa has been reduced to destitution and starvation by racially motivated land grabs. Economic mismanagement which far surpassed that of the Greeks led to an inflation rate of one million per cent.

But these outcomes scarcely rate a mention, in contrast to the global swamping of social media occasioned by the shooting of a lion.

In cyber society, there is in general only a tenuous connection between the objective content of an incident and the amount of popular attention which it receives. It is not a matter of people gathering all available information and then making a considered, rational choice, as standard economic theory assumes they do. Popularity is self-reinforcing, in a dramatic way.

Network theory is beginning to illuminate why some stories or products spread like wildfire while most receive virtually no attention. But this is due to subtle mathematical properties of the connections rather than to content or the competing merits of the product.

Economics does much better at understanding the second aspect of the Cecil story. There is a big demand across the world to hunt exotic and dangerous species. The markets for trophies and other by-products of hunting, such as the alleged aphrodisiac of powdered rhinoceros horn, are probably even larger. Unrestricted entry into such markets would lead to what is referred to as the problem of the commons. This arises when the actions of individuals, each making decisions independently and in a rational way, generate an outcome which is bad for the group as a whole. Resources become depleted to the point of extinction.

The Nobel Laureate Elinor Ostrom spent much of her career researching how this problem is managed in contexts such as fisheries and farmlands. The existence of a well-defined community, whose members influence each other through their shared values and cultural norms, is a good indicator of success. But the urge to hunt is global, and so we face a market failure.

The regulation of hunting is one of the very few functioning aspects of the Zimbabwean state. It is a way of limiting access to rare species, and the permit fees provide the resources required to combat poaching. Calls to ban hunting are ill-informed, for this would simply magnify the problem of the commons and lead to a world in which Cecils were extinct.

5 August 2015

If it can happen to Google, who can feel safe?

The new dimension of uncertainty created for policymakers by the networks of cyber society is also the theme of this piece. There had been a very short-lived but absolutely dramatic crash in the share price of Google, even then one of the world's largest companies as measured by its market capitalisation. Trading in Google shares had to be suspended.

Such 'flash crashes' have become more frequent in recent years. We have seen, for example, a collapse of 130 points in the Dow Jones index on 23 April 2013 following a hoax tweet about an attack on the White House with the president sustaining injuries.

The dramatic crash in Google's share price and the temporary suspension of trading in the company's shares made headline news. The event was triggered by the 20 per cent year-on-year fall in profits in the third quarter of this year.

As usual, there was no shortage of explanations of why this happened – after the event! A simple search of Yahoo! Finance of more than 40 brokers shows that in the previous three months, all had recommended 'strong buy', 'buy' or 'hold'. Not a single one classed the stock as 'underperform' or 'sell'. Indeed, over the entire previous year, Google's share price had risen more or less continuously. The total increase had been around 30 per cent.

But once the collapse had happened, everything became crystal clear. It was apparent that the $12.5 billion acquisition of Motorola had been a mistake, because the cell phone manufacturer has been left behind by fashionable rivals. Further, it was obvious that advertisers were reducing their payments on click-through ads because of the switch to mobile devices by consumers.

It is good fun to mock highly paid analysts when they get things wrong. But the Google incident has much wider implications for the sort of world in which companies now have to operate.

A specific point concerning the internet is that we are still in a state of flux about how to set prices in this revolutionary medium of communication. Standard economic theory is no help at all. This tells a company to set price equal to marginal cost. In other words, to equate price to the cost of producing and selling one more item.

But for many web-based applications, the marginal cost is to all intents and purposes zero. Once your system is set up, it costs nothing when the next customer clicks on the site. Any company following this economic precept on pricing would soon go bankrupt. All we can say is that we are in a process of very rapid evolution, and no one has yet worked out a satisfactory answer on price.

The wider issue relates to corporate reputation more generally. In the highly networked and connected world in which we live, companies can be blindsided by entirely unexpected reactions to events. Google knew about Motorola and advertising rates. More importantly, Google knew that the analysts knew. But the actual reaction seems to have come as a complete surprise to everyone involved, the company and the analysts.

The publication of the notorious cartoons of Muhammad in Denmark attracted little attention, despite vociferous protests from Danish Muslims. Four months later, the Muslim world erupted in reaction to them.

This inherent uncertainty about which stories will gain traction and in what way is a deep feature of networked systems. Systems in which people react to the reactions of other people. Even small-scale events or an adverse comment on a blog have the potential to go viral. Understanding and managing reputation in this new, emerging world is a major challenge for all companies.

24 October 2012

Um Bongo: a spotlight on modern social and economic behaviour

Attention spans and memories have certainly shortened during the 2010s, the decade in which cyber society effectively came of age. This article focuses on these shortenings, though the piece itself was inspired by a survey on the 60th anniversary of commercial television in the UK which documented the longevity of an advertising jingle from the 1980s.

Readers who either had young children or were children themselves in the 1980s will recall the Um Bongo jingle. The advert assured us it was drunk in the Congo. A survey published last week to mark the 60th anniversary of British television advertising showed that no fewer than 32 per cent of the total sample of 2,000 people remembered the tune. This compared to only 20 per cent who identified Mozart's *Eine Kleine Nachtmusik*.

We might attribute this to the failures of our educational system to promote grand culture. But despite Justin Bieber selling more than 15 million albums and having almost 70 million Twitter followers, only 19 per cent of those polled could name his recent number one hit.

In contrast to both high and low music culture, Um Bongo has seared itself into the brain cells. The failure of four out of five people to remember even the name of the

Bieber song could perhaps be due to the age profile of his target audience. But their parents can hardly fail to be aware of him, in the same way that they knew of a drink which few of them actually consumed.

A potential reason for the differences is that the turnover in popular cultural markets has speeded up decisively in recent years. Attention spans have shortened.

The changes in technology have made it very hard to make direct comparisons over the history of popular music charts since the early 1950s. But the trend was already apparent when the *New Musical Express* charts, introduced in 1952, were discontinued in 2006.

The early and mid 1960s were a highly innovative period, with the emergence of, for example, the Beatles and the Rolling Stones. There were also many one-hit wonders seeking to emulate their success. At this time, in terms of the Top 75 in the NME charts, around 300 songs featured during the course of each year.

By the mid 1980s, this figure has doubled to some 600, and in the mid 2000s it was around 1,000. So the turnover had risen sharply even a decade ago. Songs were getting less and less time to imprint themselves on memories. And there were many more of them which did become popular, even for a short time, so the competition to capture memory intensified.

A dramatic rise in 'churn', the speed at which relative popularity changes, can also be seen since 2000 in the choice of baby names, both here and in the US.

Baby names may seem frivolous, but the polymath American psychologist Steven Pinker emphasises their cultural importance. The choice of name 'encapsulates the great contradiction in human life: between the desire to fit in and the desire to be unique'. In the last decade or so, the latter has strengthened dramatically. The Houston anthropologist Alex Bentley and I have published papers showing that turnover in popularity was steady for most of the twentieth century, but has since risen fivefold.

Attention spans have shortened, with important consequences for our society and economy. But, for some at least, Um Bongo lives forever.

30 September 2015

Popular culture is the driving force of inequality

Our cyber world is increasingly dominated by feedback, with self-reinforcing processes (Ormerod 2012; Watts 2002). Once a topic or a behaviour becomes adopted by enough people, even more people take it up simply because it is popular.

The Oscars are a good example. In a highly networked world, huge inequalities of outcomes almost become the norm. Policymakers have hardly begun to face up to the implications of this.

The Oscars have come and gone for another year. Winning an Oscar is very often the basis for either making a fortune, or turning an existing one into mega riches. Jack Nicholson has an estimated worth of over $400 million, and stars like Tom Hanks and Robert de Niro are not far behind.

Even winners who lack the instant recognition of these stars do not do too badly. Cuba Gooding Jr has recently starred in the American civil rights film *Selma*. But after his 1996 Oscar for a supporting role in *Jerry Maguire*, he became notorious among film buffs for appearing in movies which were panned by critics and which tanked commercially. This has not stopped his wealth rising to an estimated $40 million.

The Premier League has provided us with another example of success apparently reinforcing success. Its recent TV deal with Sky and BT Sports is worth over £5 billion. Along with investment banking, soccer is one of the few industries which practices socialism, with almost all the income of the companies eventually ending up in the hands of what we might call the workers. The year immediately prior to the financial crisis, 2007, still represents a high point in the annual earnings of many people. But the average salary of a Premier League player has risen over this period from some £750,000 to almost £2.5 million.

At one level, films and football seem to provide ammunition for the sub-Marxist arguments of people like Thomas Piketty, arguing that capitalism inevitably leads to greater inequality. The rich simply get richer. This conveniently ignores the fact that over the fifty years between around 1920 and 1970, there was a massive movement towards greater equality in the West, in both income and wealth.

During the second half of the twentieth century, a profound difference in communications technology opened up between the world as it is now and all previous human history. Television by the 1960s had become more or less ubiquitous in the West. Vast numbers of people could access the same visual information at the same time. The internet has of course enormously increased the connectivity of virtually the whole world.

These advances in technology have altered the way in which people respond to information. The importance of social networks in influencing the choices made by individuals has risen sharply. The economic model of choice in which rational individuals carefully sift all the available information is no longer even feasible in many situations. Almost all click throughs on Google searches, for example, are on the first three sites which come up. It is simply not possible to work through the thousands, or even millions, of sites which are offered.

This means that self-reinforcing processes are set up. Things which become popular become even more popular, simply because they are popular. And because of communications technology, we know what is popular. In popular culture, a rapidly growing sector of the economy embracing both films and soccer, high levels of inequality of income are inevitable.

25 February 2015

What the Emily Thornberry saga tells us about macroeconomic policy

The last piece of the section serves as a link to the next section of this book, which is on macroeconomics. It highlights the importance in cyber society of narratives, and how they either spread or are contained across the relevant networks of agents.

The legal spokesperson for the Labour Party, Emily Thorn-berry, had been forced to resign from her post in the Shadow Cabinet. A condescending tweet in which she had disrespected a huge England flag draped on a working-class house had gone viral. Previously, however, despite her own privileged upbringing, she had succeeded in creating a narrative within the Labour Party of having a humble background.

There is a direct link with macroeconomics, where it is also the case that the narrative which evolves around an event is even more important than the facts. The example of the Coalition UK government creating the narrative of fiscal prudence and stability is given.

It has been a wretched week for Emily Thornberry. The high-flying MP for Islington was sacked as Shadow Attorney General and widely pilloried in both social media and conventional newsprint for tweeting a picture of a white van and England flags in Strood. Yet the saga tells us more about perception, about the narrative which emerges around a story, than about the objective reality of the event itself.

One of Thornberry's defences was that she had grown up on a council estate, and so was very familiar with the world of the working class. She had indeed successfully presented an image of herself within the Labour Party of having a humble background. This was no disadvantage in her rise, in the so-called People's Party, to a position of being a close ally of its Leader. However, her Wikipedia entry paints a subtly different picture. Her father was a successful academic, who went on to become United Nations

Assistant Secretary General. Her mother was a teacher and mayor of their local town. Image triumphed over reality.

Her misdemeanour is an even more striking example of the importance of perception. It was a week in which the England football team had played and won two matches. Imagine if Nigel Farage, the UKIP leader, had tweeted an image of the now famous white van and the three national flags draped over the house. Suppose further that the former stockbroker had posted the identical comment 'I've never seen anything like it in my life'.

Now, we will never know for certain what his reception would have been. But it seems plausible that it would have been seen as a eulogy to patriotism and to the success of our boys on the field. Instead, Thornberry was ridiculed as a patronising snob. Exactly the same actual event, completely different consequences.

The impact of macroeconomic policy shares this same characteristic. The narrative which evolves around an event is even more important than the facts. It was a great coup by David Cameron and George Osborne in the aftermath of the 2010 general election to succeed in presenting the government as being financially prudent.

It is even more impressive that the markets still believe them. On coming to power over four years ago, the government projected that borrowing in the current financial year, 2014/15, would be just under £40 billion. It is on track to be around £100 billion. What is more, over the first seven months of this financial year, borrowing is even higher than it was in 2013/14. The increase is not great, £3.7 billion according to the Office for National Statistics, but it is still up, not down. The stock of outstanding government debt sits at around 80 per cent of GDP, a figure similar to that of Spain.

Against this, the government suffers politically for what is believed to be its austerity programme, one which scarcely exists in reality. The increasing importance of perception and narrative confound the attempts by mainstream economics to build mechanistic models of the economy.

26 November 2014

References

Del Vicario, M., Bessi, A., Zollo, F., Petroni, F., Scala, A., Caldarelli, G., Stanley, H. E. and Quatrociocchi, W. (2015) The spreading of misinformation online. *Proceedings of the National Academy of Sciences* 113(3): 554–559 (doi: 10.1073/pnas.1517441113).

Lucifora, C. and Tonello, M. (2015) Cheating and social interactions. Evidence from a randomized experiment in a national evaluation program. *Journal of Economic Behaviour and Organization* 115: 45–66. (This is the journal publication of the original working paper I read in 2012.)

Ormerod, P. (2012) *Positive Linking: How Networks and Incentives Can Revolutionise the World.* London: Faber and Faber.

Ostrom, E. (2009) Beyond markets and states: polycentric governance of complex economic systems. Nobel Prize lecture (https://www.nobelprize.org/nobel_prizes/economic-sciences/laureates/2009/ostrom_lecture.pdf).

Schelling, T. C. (1971) Dynamic models of segregation. *Journal of Mathematical Sociology* 1(2): 143–86.

Schelling, T. C. (1973) Hockey helmets, concealed weapons, and daylight saving: a study of binary choices with externalities. *Journal of Conflict Resolution* 17(3): 381–428.

Schelling, T. C. (2005) Nobel Prize lecture (https://www.nobelprize.org/nobel_prizes/economic-sciences/laureates/2005/schelling-lecture.pdf).

Watts, D. (2002) A simple model of global cascades on random networks. *Proceedings of the National Academy of Sciences* 99(9): 5766–71.

6 MACROECONOMICS

The legions of economists employed by governments, regulatory agencies and central banks occupy most of their time doing microeconomics. They are busy examining the impacts of specific incentives, thinking about how to adjust particular tax rates, designing rules and regulations for various markets. It is very influential work. But for the most part, it takes place behind the scenes.

It is macro which is the public face of economics. It is the City economist wheeled out on the television news to give his or her opinion on an economic statistic which has just been published. It is the forecasts for things like GDP growth, inflation and the public sector deficit which form the centrepiece of the Chancellor's budget statements.

It was the focus of the Queen's famous question to the faculty of the London School of Economics when she visited the distinguished institution in early November 2008. The financial crisis was almost at its peak, following the collapse of Lehman Brothers in September that year. During a briefing by the academics, she asked: 'Why did nobody notice it?'

The director of research in the LSE management centre replied, without a trace of irony: 'At every stage, someone was relying on somebody else and everyone thought they were doing the right thing.'

As discussed in the Introduction, within mainstream economics there is a great deal of consensus about micro-economics. There may be disagreements about the empirical impact of, say, a change in a particular tax rate. But the way in which the analysis should be done, and the theoretical approaches to the problem will command broad assent within the profession.

This is most certainly not the case within macroeconomics. There is in fact a dominant school of thought in academic circles. But it does not command agreement across the profession in the same way that the school of thought based upon rational choice does in microeconomics.

These mainstream models rejoice in the splendid, if incomprehensible to the non-economist, title of 'dynamic stochastic general equilibrium' (DSGE). The seminal work was carried out by the American academics Finn Kydland and Edward Prescott in the 1980s. They were awarded the Nobel Prize for it in 2004.

To the general public, DSGE models are invisible. But they are very influential in central banks and finance ministries. So it is worth taking a bit of time to convey some basic background about them.

DSGE models involve heavy-duty maths. Typically, students will not encounter them until the final year of their undergraduate courses, and often not until they undertake graduate work. They are regarded as being at the intellectual cutting edge of economics.

But, almost incredibly, they make the simplifying assumption that there is only one agent in the entire economy, what is known in economics as the 'representative agent'.[1]

All scientific theories make simplifying assumptions. This one might be seen already as a step too far. If there is only one agent, we cannot, for example, have someone who is a creditor and another agent who is a debtor. Little wonder these models struggled to cope with the financial crisis, when credit and debt became paramount.

During the past three or four decades, microeconomics has moved forward a long way in developing more realistic approaches to agent behaviour. Ironically, over the same period, the self-imposed task of the macro mainstream has been to incorporate an outdated version of the rational agent into their models.

The essential task facing the 'representative' agent – and I am not making this up – is decide how best to allocate its time between work and leisure, not just now, but into the infinite future. The agent acts in complete accord with the principles of rational behaviour.

Without going into the grisly details, an implication of the theoretical model is that the agent is never unemployed. In some periods, it may seem to be, for the simple reason that it is doing no work. But that is just a choice it has made between work and leisure.

---

1 Very recent versions include more than one, but the total number remains very small.

Even within the profession itself, the DSGE models are seen by some prominent academics as simply bizarre. Paul Krugman, for example, famously said that the models implied that the 25 per cent unemployment experienced in the US in the Great Depression of the 1930s was simply a result of a mass decision to take a long vacation.

Nevertheless, these models are seen by many economists to be a major advance in scientific understanding. Robert Lucas of Chicago, for example, is a major figure in the world of rational, equilibrium macroeconomics. He was awarded the Nobel Prize for 'having transformed macroeconomic analysis and deepened our understanding of economic policy' using this kind of analysis.

In his presidential address to the American Economic Association in 2003 Lucas claimed that 'the central problem of depression-prevention has been solved.'

Olivier Blanchard is a former chief economist at the International Monetary Fund. Just three weeks before the collapse of Lehman Brothers in September 2008, he published an MIT Discussion Paper surveying the state of macroeconomics. He praised the fact that the theoretical 'battles' in macroeconomics of yesteryear were well and truly over. Everyone, except a few incorrigible dissenters, now viewed macroeconomics through the lens of rational, equilibrium behaviour. Only days before the world financial system almost collapsed completely, he pronounced that 'the state of macro is good'.

Blanchard also pointed out that DSGE models had not merely captured the support of the academic profession, but central banks as well: 'nearly every central bank', he wrote, 'either has one or wants one.'

We might usefully ask here whether the central banks were exercising independent, rational choice in their decisions to adopt DSGE models, or whether they were merely copying each other and following a fashion. But the fact is that, regardless of how they chose, they all wanted one.

Incredibly, these models still prosper. A huge amount of effort since the financial crisis has gone into introducing sufficient sand into their smooth-running equilibrium machinery to enable the models to generate an actual recession. When the Queen asked her question, they simply could not.

No surprise, then, that they did not see the crisis coming and that, to repeat the words of the president of the European Central Bank cited in the Introduction, during the crisis policymakers felt 'abandoned' by the mainstream models.

Outside the charmed circle of DSGE devotees, there is still a great deal of dissent within macroeconomics. At the height of the financial crisis in the autumn of 2008, one group of economists believed that the banks should be rescued, while another argued that they should be allowed to go under. Both groups included Nobel Laureates.

In terms of contemporary policy, should governments, for example, abandon 'austerity' by spending more and running up bigger deficits and building up more public-sector debt? Should interest rates be increased, following the record-breaking length of time they have remained at very low levels? Support both for and against these propositions can be found within the economics profession.

Macroeconomics is a good illustration of the limits to knowledge. Despite intensive efforts over many decades, not much progress has been made in terms of understanding how the economy operates at the macro level.

One manifestation of this is the very poor record of economic forecasting. A recent example is the prediction made by the Treasury during the Brexit referendum in the summer of 2016. If the UK voted Leave, unemployment was forecast to rise by half a million by the end of 2016. At the time of writing, at the end of 2017, it has in fact fallen to its lowest level in over 40 years.

Want an economic forecast guv?
Pick one, any one will do

The Office for Budget Responsibility (OBR) is the independent body set up by the coalition government of 2010–15 to provide macroeconomic assessments for the government. In late 2016, the government was coming under pressure after the OBR had released a set of forecasts which were slightly more pessimistic than their previous ones.

In the US, the Survey of Professional Forecasters has a track record of predictions going back 50 years.[2] Even just four quarters ahead, the average prediction of GDP growth made by professional forecasters has a correlation with the actual growth rate of, literally, zero. And there is no sign that the accuracy has improved over time.

Economic forecasts have become a political hot potato. The Office for Budget Responsibility's predictions, presented as part of the Chancellor's Autumn Statement, have put the government under pressure. The OBR has revised down its forecast for GDP growth over the next four years by 1.4 percentage points.

The real controversy is because their gloomy projections for GDP and the government finances have been placed at the door of Brexit. In the simple phrase of the OBR: 'Any likely Brexit outcome would lead to lower potential output'. Lower output leads to lower tax receipts, and worse government finances

---

2   https://www.philadelphiafed.org/research-and-data/real-time-center/survey-of-professional-forecasters/

To be fair, the OBR do say that 'in current circumstances the uncertainty around the forecasts is even greater than it would be in normal times'. But just how great is this uncertainty?

Studies are published from time to time about the accuracy of economic forecasts. The best set of records is kept in America, though the less systematic evidence for the UK shows that the track records are very similar in the two countries.

The Survey of Professional Forecasters (SPF) collects the forecasts on variables such as GDP growth and inflation from a wide range of forecasters. Their database goes back almost 50 years, to 1968. Just one quarter ahead, the predictions are *on average* completely accurate. 'One quarter ahead' means the next three months, so at the moment it would refer to the period January to March 2017.

This average accuracy conceals errors in most forecasts for any particular quarter, the errors cancel out over time. For example, the quarter from July to September 2008 marked the onset of the major recession of the financial crisis. At an annual rate, GDP fell by 1.9 per cent compared to the previous quarter. But the SPF predictions made in the April to June period for July to September were for growth of 0.7 per cent.

The SPF predictions account for only 25 per cent of the variability around the average. When we go four quarters ahead – just one year – the predictions are even worse. Negative growth, for example, has never been predicted, even though there have been 26 quarters of negative growth since 1968.

The track record, which has not got any better over time, shows that in relatively calm times, forecasts just one year ahead have a reasonable degree of accuracy. But when major changes are taking place, just when they are really needed, they have none.

The OBR cannot be blamed for producing predictions four years ahead when the track record of the forecasting community shows them to be of no value. That is what George Osborne mandated them to do when he set the independent body up in 2010. But four years ahead, almost any set of predictions is just as good – or bad – as another.

It would be much better to abolish the OBR and restore responsibility to the Treasury and, ultimately, to the politicians. If they get it wrong and are too optimistic, we can at least kick them out.

30 November 2016

What a good job Keynes didn't believe in forecasting

Substantial errors in prediction have a long history, going back at least as far as Keynes himself.

Writing in the Times in 1933, during the Great Depression, he struck a very pessimistic note, and called for a major change of policy. But, almost immediately, the economy began a very strong and spontaneous recovery.

Keynes should not really have been surprised. As we saw in the section on uncertainty and the limits to knowledge, he himself believed strongly in the inherent difficulties of making successful predictions.

Keynes is in many people's minds at the moment. Uncertainty about the course of the economy is high. Nobel prizewinning economist Paul Krugman is filling the media with calls for governments to spend more and increase their deficits.

The 1930s and the Great Depression are often mentioned in this context. Surely, it is asserted, these are the policies which saved us then, so let's have them now. But, quite simply, it is an urban myth.

In May 1933, at roughly the same stage in the cycle as we are today, Keynes wrote in *The Times*: 'Confidence has been restored and cheap money established both on long and on short term [the equivalent of zero interest rates and quantitative easing from the Bank of England today]. Yet unemployment has not declined. Where are we to look for the explanation? Not in the international sphere; for our net foreign trade position, though still bad, is much improved [the equivalent of the increase in net exports caused by the 25 per cent depreciation of sterling since 2007]. We can find it nowhere, I suggest, except in the decline in our loan expenditure, as the result of our no longer borrowing for the dole and of our restraining the capital expenditure of all public authorities'.

Keynes made the case for tax cuts and infrastructure spending to boost growth and reduce unemployment. He made it clear he had little time for fiscal masochism, noting: 'Unfortunately the more pessimistic the chancellor's policy, the more likely it is that pessimistic anticipations will be realised and vice versa. Whatever the chancellor dreams will come true!'

But despite his eloquence, Keynes did not at the time influence policy either here or in the US. 'Fiscal masochism' continued to be the dominant theme in policy.

When Keynes urged the adoption of more spending and more borrowing in 1933, the economic situation looked dire. In 1932, real GDP had grown, but by only 0.8 per cent. Unemployment was at a record high of 14 per cent.

Here is what actually happened to growth and unemployment in the UK:

	Real GDP growth (per cent)	Unemployment rate (per cent)
1933	2.9	12.7
1934	6.6	10.7
1935	3.9	9.9
1936	4.5	8.5

So, yes, no sooner had Keynes written these words that confidence was restored. Spontaneous optimism broke out despite Keynes's pessimism that a complete change of policy was needed for this to happen. The economy boomed and unemployment nearly halved. The same thing happened in the US. The economy grew even faster than in the UK, by 7.7 per cent in 1934, 7.6 per cent in 1935 and an astonishing 14.2 per cent in 1936.

The key to sustainable recovery is the private sector, and specifically companies. It is companies which innovate, which carry out investment, which create jobs. Many of Europe's large companies are sitting on massive piles of cash; their balance sheets are strong. If confidence is restored in the corporate sector, this cash will be spent and we will see growth rates similar to those of the mid 1930s.

Of course, the fact that corporate sentiment recovered in the 1930s and generated a boom is no guarantee that the same will happen again. But what is needed for this is a stable framework, with no surprises.

The European Commission and countries such as France, Spain and Italy need to come clean on the position of their banks. The emergence of bad news in dribs and drabs has a wholly negative effect on confidence. We need to know the true position, regardless of the *amour propre* and pride of the ruling elites in these countries.

Of course, people usually only want to be told the truth by their doctors if the news is good. But getting everything out into the open is a much better strategy than the veil of secrecy and the wringing out of the truth which has actually happened.

6 June 2012

Inflation and the limits to knowledge

Central banks around the world are charged with controlling the level of inflation. Around 20 years ago, the vogue among policymakers was to make these banks formally independent. The Bank of England was one such example, being made independent by the then finance minister, Gordon Brown.

Over this time, inflation has indeed been low, leading many economists to proclaim this as a triumph of their expertise.

173

The reality is quite different. Inflation is low for other reasons, and the standard theory used by economists to understand inflation is simply not compatible with the empirical evidence.

Mark Carney, Governor of the Bank of England, is getting his retaliation in early. Faced yet again with the Bank failing to deliver its designated target of a 2 per cent inflation rate, in a speech last week he suggested that his remit was broader.

'We face a trade-off between having inflation above target and the need to support, or the desirability of supporting, jobs and activity', the Governor stated.

In other words, he claimed that the Monetary Policy Committee (MPC) of the Bank should be concerned not just with inflation, but with what economists describe as the 'real' economy, output and jobs.

The Federal Reserve in the US is explicitly mandated to take account of both inflation and the real economy when it sets interest rates. This is definitely not the case with the Bank of England. When Gordon Brown made it independent in 1997, its remit was unequivocal. It was to ensure that inflation was 2 per cent a year.

This time round inflation is above the Bank's target. The current level of some 3 per cent may even rise in the short term because the weakness of sterling is pushing up the cost of imports.

But in recent years, inflation has been below the 2 per cent desired rate, even falling to zero in 2015.

And all this time, the Bank rate has been essentially flat. The MPC cut it to just 0.5 per cent in March 2009, where it remained until the reduction to 0.25 per cent in August 2016.

To put this into perspective, when the rate fell to 1.5 per cent in January 2009, this was the first time it had been below 2 per cent since the Bank was created in 1694, well over 300 years ago.

So here is a puzzle for mainstream macroeconomists, whether in central banks or universities. Central banks are meant in theory to be able to control inflation by setting short-term interest rates. Inflation has been low since 2009. But at the same time the Bank rate has been at all-time record lows.

Perhaps more pertinently, inflation has fluctuated from year to year, even though interest rates have to all intents and purposes not changed. It was 4.5 per cent in 2011, and 0.7 per cent in 2016.

In short, inflation seems to lead a life of its own, independently of what the experts on the MPC either say or do.

Inflation really is a naughty boy all round. A central concept in orthodox economic thinking, encapsulated in the quote from Mark Carney above, is that there is a trade-off between inflation and jobs and output. The faster the economy grows and unemployment falls, the higher will be inflation.

But starting in the early 1990s, for around 15 years across the entire Western world both inflation and unemployment experienced prolonged falls.

The idea that a central bank can control inflation by adjusting interest rates is shown by the evidence to be absurd. It is yet another example of the limits to knowledge in orthodox macroeconomics.

25 October 2017

A tale of two crises

What we saw in the 1930s was the revival of Keynes's animal spirits, of the percolation across the relevant networks of a more optimistic narrative about the future. Exactly the same phenomenon has been seen in the recovery from the second global financial crisis of the past 150 years, that of the late 2000s.[3]

Despite gloomy prognostications from metropolitan liberal commentators about the strength of the recovery, the piece of shows that the recovery this time round is comparable to, and in some ways better than, the revival which took place in the 1930s.

Ten years ago, the financial crisis began to grip the Western economies. During the course of 2007, GDP growth slowed markedly everywhere. By the end of 2008, output was in free fall.

A key theme in economic commentary is the sluggishness of the subsequent recovery of the developed economies.

---

3   An excellent source of historical data is the works of Angus Maddison (see, for example, Maddison 1995; see also http://www.theworldeconomy.org/).

The picture is not quite as bad as it is usually painted. True, last week the Office for National Statistics announced a dip in UK growth in the first quarter of this year. But from 2009, the trough of the recession, to 2016, GDP growth averaged 2.0 per cent a year. Not exactly a stellar performance.

But from 1973, the year prior to the major oil price shock, to 2007, the British economy expanded by just 2.3 per cent a year on average. The contrast between the two periods in the US is slightly greater. From 1973 to 2007, growth averaged 3.0 per cent a year, and since 2009 it has been 2.1 per cent.

There is a very stark contrast with the experience of the 1930s, the last time there was a global financial crisis. This time is different: things have only got better. The recovery may be slower than desirable, but it has been much more widespread than in the years following the Great Depression of the 1930s.

A decisive indicator is the length of time it took not just for growth to resume, but for the previous peak level of GDP to be regained. So in the UK, for example, the economy started to grow again in 2010. But it was not until 2013 that there had been enough growth for the economy to get back to its 2007 size.

Looking at a group of 18 developed economies, which includes all the main and medium-sized ones, GDP had regained its previous peak within three years in no fewer than eight of them. By 2016, everyone in the group except Finland, Italy and Spain had a GDP which exceeded its previous peak.

Three years after output began to fall in 1930, not a single economy had managed to regain its 1929 level of output. Even by 1938, output was below its 1929 level in Austria, Canada, France, the Netherlands, Switzerland and Spain.

Perhaps Keynes's most powerful insight was why the slump was so prolonged. He developed the concept of 'animal spirits', which are not a mathematically based prediction of the future, but the sentiment of the narratives which companies form about the future. He wrote: 'the essence of the situation is to be found in the collapse of animal spirits … this may be so complete that no practicable reduction in the rate of interest will be enough.'

Zero interest rates and low growth! Keynes got there before us.

Still, capitalism has performed much better in the aftermath of the financial crisis of the late 2000s than it did in the crisis of the early 1930s. Animal spirits may not be buoyant, but they are in much better shape than in the 1930s.

3 May 2017

The private sector, not the state, drives America's recovery

There have been many strident calls since the financial crisis to 'end austerity'. Government spending should be increased and paid for by the government running a large deficit and paying for it by issuing more debt.

There is good evidence to suggest, however, that not only is this unnecessary given the recovery in the economy, but that it could be positively dangerous.

The economic recovery, both in the UK and in America, has taken place even though 'austerity' has been in place.

The American economy continues to power ahead. The widely respected and independent Congressional Budget Office (CBO) reckons that the actual level of GDP in the US in 2017 is finally back at the level of potential output.

The potential level of GDP is the amount of output which would be produced if there were no spare capacity in the economy. In a service- and internet-oriented economy, any estimates of it are fraught with difficulties.

The maximum output of a car plant or steel mill is reasonably straightforward to work out, at least in the short term. But it is less obvious what the constraints are on any web-related business.

Still, the concept of potential output is taken seriously by policymakers. And the CBO does a better job than most at guessing what it is.

On their figures, the last time actual and potential GDP were in balance was in the year immediately prior to the crisis, 2007, which at least makes sense. In 2009, the depth of the recession, the CBO calculates the gap between the two to be 6 per cent. That may not sound a lot, but in money terms that represents more than one trillion dollars.

American GDP is now almost 15 per cent more than it was in 2007, and 20 per cent more than in 2009.

Along with this, employment has surged, with 17.2 million net new jobs being created from the low point of December 2009. As in the UK, employment is at record highs.

The increase in employment is entirely due to the private sector, where it has grown by 17.3 million. In contrast, the numbers employed by the government, whether federal or state, have been cut by 100,000.

The same applies on the output side. Again, it is the private sector which is driving the recovery.

Compared to the bottom of the recession in 2009, and after stripping out inflation, public sector spending is down by $200 billion. In contrast, private sector investment has risen more than 10 times this amount, an increase of $2.1 trillion.

So, despite strict restraints on the public sector, the American economy has recovered well from the crisis. Indeed, better than the best-performing main European economies, Germany and the UK.

The evidence has been there all along, as soon as the US began to pull out of the recession in the early part of this decade. It is evidence which seems to be studiously ignored by the strident voices in British academic circles calling for an end to 'austerity'.

Of course, there have been tax cuts, and these stimulate the private sector. But the risk over the longer term is that growth will not be rapid enough to bring in enough revenue to curb the growth in public sector debt.

Indeed, the CBO sees the potential rise in this debt as an important threat to the long-term growth of America. Higher public borrowing, in its view, reduces the private sector investment which is needed for growth.

6 December 2017

Cutting spending *can* be expansionary

This piece was written three years after the previous one, and focuses on the UK. The evidence again supports the idea that austerity can expand the economy (Congdon 2015; Barro 1974; Alesina and Ardagna 2010).

The key aim of George Osborne's economic policy has been to eliminate the financial deficit of the public sector. The main way of trying to achieve this has been to squeeze public spending. The orthodox economic textbooks maintain that this withdraws demand from the economy, and so leads to the growth rate being slower than it would otherwise be.

But can contractionary fiscal policy of this kind actually expand the economy? At first sight, it seems something of a contradiction, the concept that spending less might cause higher growth. An oxymoron, one might say – where I am using the word in its regular sense and not referring to those Greeks who voted 'no' in the referendum. The very idea provokes howls of derision and outrage, from leading Keynesians such as Stiglitz and Krugman downwards.

Yet we have been here before. In early 1981, the UK economy had moved into a deep recession, comparable in size to that which we experienced during the financial crisis. In the budget of March of that year, the then Chancellor, Geoffrey Howe, cut the financial deficit by 1.5 per cent of GDP, or some £20 billion in today's prices.

This prompted no fewer than 364 university economists to write to *The Times* in protest, explaining that the policy was completely misguided and would only serve to prolong the recession. In fact, the economy began to recover during 1981, and posted a healthy growth rate of 2.2 per cent in 1982, followed by a boom rate of 3.9 per cent in 1983.

One swallow does not make a summer. Is there any other evidence? Tim Congdon, in a recent article in the journal *Economic Affairs*, claims that since the 1980s, 'expansionary fiscal contractions' have been the norm rather than the exception both in the UK and the US. Keynesian support for fiscal activism is, he argues, unsupported by a large body of recent evidence.

To cite just one example, Congdon points to the substantial fiscal tightening under the Conservatives from 1994 and initially continued by Gordon Brown until 2000. Over this period, the UK economy grew rapidly.

There are good theoretical reasons for thinking that cutting the government deficit could stimulate rather than contract the economy. The classic paper was written by Robert Barro of Harvard as long ago as 1974. Its rather mysterious title, 'Are government bonds net wealth?', has not prevented it from becoming one of the most cited papers in the whole of economics.

Barro essentially argued that a nation cannot make itself better off by increasing its public debt. More recently, the work of the Italian economist Alberto Alesina, now also based at Harvard, has been influential in policymaking circles in the European Commission and European Central Bank.

The simple view that more government spending boosts the economy appears to make common sense. The opposing views are more subtle and complex. But it is the latter which at present have the upper hand.

12 August 2015

Is this a pleb I see before me?
Reality and perception in the markets

Narratives are of great importance in macroeconomics. Quite separately, a leading member of the British government, Andrew Mitchell, had been involved in an altercation with the police officers who guard the entrance to Downing Street. Rather like Emily Thornberry, the Labour politician we met in the section on networks, Mr Mitchell had an air of de haut en bas about him. It did not help that he was alleged to have described the police as 'plebs'. But, regardless of objective reality, the public narrative turned against him and he was obliged to resign.

The piece draws a parallel between this and the government's ability to sustain the narrative in financial markets that it was prudent and responsible, despite presiding over increases in public sector spending. The work of Reinhart and Rogoff on public sector debt is cited (Reinhart and Rogoff 2009). Although an error was subsequently discovered in one of their calculations, their general conclusions remain valid.

Andrew Mitchell, the Government Chief Whip, remains in some difficulty after his exchange with the police at the gates of Downing Street. At the heart of the incident, there is an objective reality. Either he used the word pleb, or he didn't. Either the police were officious jobsworths, or they were the epitome of politeness.

But perception matters much more than reality. It is perhaps unfortunate for Mitchell that he went to Rugby, the home of *Tom Brown's Schooldays* and the arrogant bully Flashman.

This wholly fictional setting and these wholly fictional characters have played an important role in shaping how many people regard the incident.

After allowing for one-offs such as the transfer of pension assets from the Royal Mail, public borrowing is actually 22 per cent higher in the April–August period than it was in the same months last year. So the deficit-reducing Osborne is actually presiding over a sharp increase in government borrowing. Yet the markets continue to believe in him, to have faith that he is committed to deficit reduction.

In terms of economic policy, the objective difference between the policies of George Osborne and Ed Balls[4] is minute. Osborne wants to achieve his target for deficit reduction in six years. Balls has the radical (!) alternative of getting to the same number in seven.

The margins of error involved in forecasts of public spending and receipts even one year ahead are huge. And the potential errors around the projected deficit, the difference between these two numbers, are even larger. The difficulties of making accurate forecasts on the deficit are illustrated by the outcome to date during the current financial year.

---

4   The economics spokesman for the Labour Party.

Given the size of potential errors around forecasts, to all intents and purposes there is no effective difference between the strategies of Balls and Osborne. Yet Balls struggles to gain credibility in financial markets. Narrative and perception outweigh reality.

This Time Is Different, the monumental study of government debt by Carmen Reinhart and Ken Rogoff, ex-Chief Economist at the IMF, showed that when public sector debt to GDP ratios rise above the 90 to 100 per cent mark, there is a sharply increased risk of both lower economic growth and of a default taking place on the debt. The data show only too clearly that the Germans are hovering very close to this critical value. Yet they are perceived as being the epitome of financial stability.

A great deal of economic policy in Europe at the moment can be seen as an attempt by various players to get their narrative of events to 'go viral' and dominate financial markets, almost regardless of objective reality.

This is the future of macroeconomics. With a real basket case such as Greece, the facts are so glaring that they will be hard to ignore. But in general, as with the Andrew Mitchell incident, they are usually capable of more than one interpretation. Perception trumps reality.

26 September 2012

How big is my multiplier?

The whole argument about austerity in recent years has essentially revolved around the size of the multiplier, a concept introduced by Keynes in his 1936 General Theory.

The question is the following. If the economy is not at full employment and the government increases spending, and hence its financial deficit, what will be the eventual impact on the output of the economy as whole?

Keynes had a much deeper understanding of the economy than most of his modern-day followers. He was very careful to qualify the potential effects of increased government spending.

Keynes raised the point that psychological factors, and in particular 'confidence', might be affected in ways which would offset the effects of an increase in government spending. Specifically, he said: 'With the confused psychology which often prevails, the government programme may, through its effect on "confidence" … retard other investment'.

But despite many decades of intensive statistical work in the area, the size of the multiplier has not been pinned down (Laury et al. 1978; Ramey 2013; Barro and Redlick 2011). Considerable uncertainty surrounds its empirical value in any particular set of circumstances. The one thing we do know is that it is, at best, low.

The debate rages about whether the Chancellor should implement a Plan B, or C or D or even Z. There seems to be a plethora of alternatives. But many of them share a key common theme. Namely, that an increase in public spending will boost output in the economy overall.

This was one of the revolutionary new ideas developed by Keynes, which he called the 'multiplier'. An increase in public spending means that more people are employed, for example in building infrastructure. These in turn spend more money and the effect ripples across the economy. The final impact is a multiple – hence the word 'multiplier' – of the initial increase in spending.

This seems to be common sense. But common sense can often lead us astray. It seems to be common sense that the Sun goes round the Earth, it goes round the sky after all. What does modern economics have to say about the size of the multiplier?

Keynes himself thought it was between 2 and 3. So an increase of £1 billion in public spending would eventually increase GDP by between £2 and £3 billion.

Great news if this is true. The tax take from an increase in spending is around 40 per cent, and 40 per cent of £2 or £3 billion is around £1 billion. So public spending creates jobs, boosts output and pays for itself.

Here is the bad news. Modern estimates of the multiplier put it much lower than that. In the late 1970s, I was involved in the first systematic comparison of the multiplier in the three leading macroeconomic models of the UK economy, including that of the Treasury. We estimated then it was between 0.5 and 1.2.

The *Journal of Economic Literature*, one of the world's top academic journals, published a symposium in September last year on the size of the multiplier. Even the Keynesian-based models of the US economy only put the multiplier at between 0.8 and 1.5. And this will be lower for much more open economies such as the UK, because a bigger proportion of any increase in spending simply leaks out of the economy in imports. Nobel prizewinner Robert Barro argues that spending targeted to have very low import content has a multiplier of around 0.6.

Poor old multiplier, just look how small it is! Even at the optimistic end, modern economics suggests that the eventual increase in national output will hardly be any bigger than the increase in public spending. Many estimates have the eventual rise as being considerably less. There are all sorts of reasons for the tiny multiplier. Some spending disappears into imports. If interest rates rise, the value of government bonds falls and there is less wealth. Economics itself suggests that more public spending is not the panacea it is purported to be.

5 September 2012

The 'output gap': another piece of economic mumbo-jumbo

In addition to the multiplier, another important concept in current policy advice from economists lacks any sound empirical basis. This is the idea of the 'output gap'.

Essentially, the output gap is the difference between the current level of output and what would be produced if the economy were running at full capacity. It is used, for example, to form views on inflation. The lower the output gap, it is claimed, the more likely it is that inflation will rise. This is turn helps form views on interest rates. So it is an important concept.

Unfortunately, it does not make much sense in a service, and especially an internet, economy. Even in the context of a simple manufacturing plant, the piece cites evidence that it is not at all clear what the output gap is at any point in time (Murray 2014; Hendel and Spiegel 2014).

The concept of the 'output gap' is central to mainstream macroeconomics. It is not merely of academic interest. The Office for Budget Responsibility (OBR) has a specific requirement to estimate the output gap, which it defines formally as 'the difference between the current level of activity in the economy and the potential level it could sustain while keeping inflation stable'.

The output gap is a key consideration for central banks around the world. If output is well below its potential, interest rates should be kept low, to try to stimulate the economy. And a large output gap should keep inflation low. Prices are hard to put up in a depressed economy.

The task of estimating the output gap empirically is fraught with difficulties. The OBR points that there are at least three recognised ways of doing this, none of which will make sense to anyone lacking an advanced training in statistics.

So there is plenty of scope for disagreement among orthodox economists who believe in the concept. Yet rather like the medieval debates about how many angels could dance on a pin, these disputes have little meaning in the economy of the twenty first century.

The economy is not a physical object and cannot, say, be placed on a pair of scales and weighed. GDP has to be estimated, using a wide range of information. The basic principles of how to measure output were worked out in the 1930s and 1940s.

A major problem is that these principles are much more suited to an economy which, as it was at that time, is dominated by the production of goods rather than services. We can count how many Ford Model Ts have been built. It is much less clear what the outputs of Google or Facebook are.

The problems are even more acute with the concept of potential output. Many internet-based services incur substantial fixed costs in order to have just a single customer. But the additional cost of servicing the second customer, and all subsequent ones, is effectively zero. Potential output does not have much meaning in these contexts, it is not obvious what the limit might be.

A powerful blow against the concept of potential output has been published in the latest edition of the American Economic Association's journal *Applied Economics*. Igal Hendel and Yossi Spiegel document the evolution of productivity over a 12-year period in a steel mini-mill producing an unchanged product, working 24/7. The steel melt shop is almost the Platonic ideal from a national accounts perspective of output measurement. The product – steel billets – is a simple, homogeneous, internationally traded product. There was virtually no turnover in the labour force, very little new investment, and the mill worked every hour of the year.

Yet despite production conditions which were almost unchanged, output doubled over the 12-year period. As the authors note, rather drily, 'the findings suggest that capacity is not well defined, even in batch-oriented manufacturing'. Time to put the concept of potential output into the rubbish bin!

22 January 2014

We are much better off than the official statistics say

There are serious issues with how output itself is measured in a service-oriented internet economy. National accounts statisticians receive information on production and spending in current price terms. Their task is to work out how much of any change is due to inflation, and how much represents a genuine change in output. In my view, output changes have been systematically underestimated and inflation overestimated.

This piece is built around a substantial report on the measurement of the economy which had just appeared (Bean 2016). This is the Bean report, produced by a group of economists under the chairmanship of Sir Charles Bean, former Deputy Governor of the Bank of England.

The oldest surviving map of Britain was created in Canterbury a thousand years ago. Our ancestors had a good idea of how to get around. The country is depicted in its familiar shape. Understanding of the world outside Western Europe remained sketchy for centuries. The phrase 'here be dragons' was allegedly used to conceal ignorance about substantial parts of the world.

Sir Charles Bean's Independent Review of UK Economic Statistics was published last week. It is an impressive and well-argued document. But it leaves the distinct impression that the state of our knowledge about how to measure the size of the economy is not much better than that of the Canterbury map makers. The Office for National Statistics knows how to guide us around the old, familiar parts of the economy.

The second paragraph of the Bean report hones in on the dragons: 'The Review was prompted by the growing difficulty of measuring output and productivity accurately in a modern, dynamic and increasingly diverse and digital economy.'

An anecdote illustrates the point. Last week, our old washing machine finally packed up. My wife went onto the internet in the afternoon, did some searches, read some price and quality comparisons sites and blogs, and placed the order. Thanks to just-in-time stock control and vastly improved logistics, the new one was safely installed and working the next morning.

Even thirty years ago, the whole process would have required much more time and nervous energy. Perhaps writing to get catalogues, visiting retailers to inspect the machines, trudging around to compare prices, finally placing the order, and hoping that there wasn't a six week wait for your chosen model, then finding someone to instal it.

None of these savings of effort or improved quality of service appear in the national accounts. The national accounts just see a retail purchase, a delivery and an installation: exactly what they would have seen thirty years ago. Yet economic statistics are, again as Bean puts it, 'central to monitoring, understanding and managing the economy, at both national and regional levels'.

A major issue for policymakers is what has become known as the 'productivity puzzle'. Since the trough of the recession in 2009, output has grown by 12.6 per cent and employment by 7.0 per cent. So productivity, output per worker, has only expanded by just over 5 per cent, or less than 1 per cent a year.

By historical standards, this is pitifully low, especially during a period of economic recovery. Companies need to be sure that demand is growing before they take people on, so employment growth lags behind output growth and productivity rises sharply. Or, at least, it did in every other recovery since World War II.

The Nobel Laureate Bob Solow, still going strong in his 90s, presciently remarked as long ago as 1987: 'You can see the computer age everywhere but in the productivity statistics'. We can rely on employment data, based as it is on PAYE returns to HMRC. But the Bean report implies we have been grossly underestimating output in the digital economy.

16 March 2016

Economists are not impressed by Piketty's views on inequality

There is much to criticise about mainstream macro. But it is not completely without its uses. The piece of draws on an excellent paper by the Cambridge economist Bob Rowthorn (2014), which used both empirics and standard theory to mount a devastating critique of Thomas Piketty's book Capital in the Twenty-First Century, which was eulogised in left-wing circles.

The financial crisis has undoubtedly created a demand in popular culture for works which portray capitalism in a bad light, such as the recent best seller by Thomas Piketty. Piketty's writing has gathered increasing attention from economists, and his arguments do not really bear scrutiny.

The focus of Piketty's work is the long-run evolution of the ratio of capital to income. He claims that this is now very high by historical standards, and will rise even further as the twenty first century unfolds. Wealth will become more concentrated and inequality will rise inexorably even more.

The message that capitalism inevitably leads to greater inequality is one that many people want to hear. Unfortunately for them, it is wrong. Piketty assembles an impressively large amount of empirical evidence. This shows clearly that from around 1910 to 1970, inequality actually declined sharply across the West.

Piketty argues that there were special factors involved in this period, which will not be repeated in the future. But modern capitalism was essentially formed in the decades either side of 1900. A truly massive merger and acquisition movement took place, and for the first time ever, companies existed which operated on a global scale.

So we have had a globalised capitalist economy for approximately 120 years. For half this period, inequality fell, and in the other half it rose. The belief that capitalism always creates inequality is scientific nonsense.

A devastating theoretical and empirical critique of Piketty is made in a recent paper by Bob Rowthorn, former head of the economics department at Cambridge. Rowthorn became in his younger days an expert in Marxist economics, and so is ideally placed to appraise Piketty's work.

Piketty shows that there has indeed been a sharp rise in the ratio of wealth to income in the early twenty first century, to around 5 or 6 compared to just 2 to 3 in the 1950s and 1960s. Rowthorn points out, using Piketty's own data, that the whole of this increase is due to capital gains in both housing and the equity markets. In real terms, the ratio has been constant in Europe and has actually fallen in America. This is highly relevant.

A crucial part of Piketty's argument about the future is that he believes that the rate of economic growth will be low. But if growth is low over many decades, it is very hard to believe that there will not be a reversal of the increases in real estate and share prices, and Piketty's measure of the ratio of wealth to income will fall.

From a theoretical perspective, mainstream economics has a great deal to say about the evolution of the ratio of capital to income, and the implications for wages and profits. Piketty uses this theory. But, as Rowthorn points out, the theory is set out in real terms, not in the current price terms which Piketty uses for his empirical evidence.

Economics can be very useful, not least in exposing the fundamental flaws in popular opinions.

9 July 2014

Capitalism is stable and resilient

A further totem of left-wing thinking about macroeconomics, prominent since the financial crisis, is that capitalism is in some way inherently unstable. It is hard to reconcile this with the evidence. There have only been two global financial crises in the past 150 years. And the average rate of unemployment in the leading Western economies has been low (Ormerod 2010).

The financial crisis did succeed in creating one dynamic new industry. Since the late 2000s, there has been a massive upsurge in op-ed pieces, books and even artistic performances offering a critique of capitalism. A founder member of the Monty Python team, Terry Jones, is the latest to get in on the act with his documentary *Boom, Bust, Boom*. The film makes use of puppetry and animation to argue that market-based economies are inherently unstable.

In the opening scene, Jones appears on Wall Street. 'This film is about the Achilles heel of capitalism', the ex-Python solemnly proclaims, 'how human nature drives the economy to crisis after crisis time and time again'.

The intellectual underpinnings of the movie are the theories of the American economist Hyman Minsky. Minsky argued that a key mechanism that pushes an economy towards a crisis is the accumulation of debt by the private sector. Although he never constructed a formal model, Minsky's ideas are clearly relevant to the run-up to the crash in 2008. They at least deserve to be taken seriously.

But does life really imitate art? Is capitalism genuinely unstable in the way in which Jones alleges in the film? An immediate problem for this view is that there have only been two global financial crashes in the past 150 years. The early 1930s and the late 2000s are the only periods in which these were experienced. So an event which takes place approximately once every 75 years is hardly convincing evidence with which to indict an entire system with the charge of instability.

One way of looking at the stability of capitalism is through the labour market. If the system experiences frequent crises, the average rate of unemployment will be high. But this does not seem to be the case.

From the end of World War II until the oil price crisis of the mid 1970s, unemployment averaged just under 5 per cent in America and was less than 3 per cent in the UK and Germany. Even during the more turbulent times since the 1970s, before the 2008/9 crisis, the unemployment rate averaged 6–7 per cent in the three economies. Higher, but by no means catastrophic given that Keynes himself thought it was very unlikely that the rate could be much less than 3 per cent over long periods of time.

It could be argued that since 1945, the state has intervened much more in the economy, and it is this which has kept unemployment low. But over the 1870–1938 period, the numbers are very similar to those seen post-war. In the US, it is 7 per cent, 5.5 per cent in Britain, and under 4 per cent in Germany.

Most recessions are in fact very short-lived. Since the late nineteenth century, 70 per cent of all recessions lasted just a single year. The distinguishing feature of capitalism is not its instability, but its resilience. Markets are not perfect, but unemployment is usually low. Crises happen, but the system bounces back.

8 April 2015

References

Alesina, A. and Ardagna, S. (2010) Large changes in fiscal policy: taxes versus spending. NBER Working Paper 15438.

Barro, R. J. (1974) Are government bonds net wealth? *Journal of Political Economy* 82(6): 1095–117.

Barro, R. J. and Redlick, C. J. (2011) Macroeconomic effects from government purchases and taxes (https://ideas.repec.org/a/oup/qjecon/v126y2011i1p51-102.html).

Bean, C. (2016) Independent Review of UK Economic Statistics: Final Report (https://www.gov.uk/government/publications/independent-review-of-uk-economic-statistics-final-report).

Congdon, T. (2015) In praise of expansionary fiscal contraction. *Economic Affairs* 35(1): 21–34.

Hendel, I. and Spiegel, Y. (2014) Small steps for workers, a giant leap for productivity. *American Economic Journal: Applied Economics* 6(1): 73–90.

Laury, J. S. E., Lewis, G. R. and Ormerod, P. A. (1978) Properties of macroeconomic models of the UK: a comparative survey. *National Institute Economic Review* 83(1): 52–72.

Maddison, A. (1995) *Monitoring the World Economy 1820–1992.* Paris: OECD.

Murray, J. (2014) Output gap measurement: judgement and uncertainty. Office for Budget Responsibility Working Paper 5.

Ormerod, P. (2010) Risk, recessions and the resilience of the capitalist economies. *Risk Management* 12(1): 83–99.

Ramey, V. A. (2013) Can government purchases stimulate the economy? *Journal of Economic Literature* 49(3): 673–85.

Reinhart, C. M. and Rogoff, K. S. (2009) *This Time Is Different: Eight Centuries of Financial Folly*. Princeton University Press.

Rowthorn, R. (2014) A note on Piketty's *Capital in the Twenty-First Century*. *Cambridge Journal of Economics* 38(5): 1275–84.

A FEW SUGGESTIONS FOR FURTHER READING

As I have mentioned several times, this is not meant to be either an economics textbook or a comprehensive guide to the literature of particular areas of economics. So this list does exactly what the heading suggests. It sets out a small number of recommendations for further reading.

Almost all of these will be accessible to the general reader. This does not mean that they are easy reads, for they deal with issues which are intellectually demanding. But even if some sections of a paper seem to require too much prior knowledge or appear particularly difficult, the general flavour of the overall arguments should come across.

The list begins with some Nobel lectures, which collectively give a good indication of how economics is making progress. Most of these have already been cited in the references following individual chapters, but are repeated here for convenience.

Nobel lectures where the recipients worked on equilibrium macroeconomics are conspicuous by their absence.

In my view, students today would benefit from reading a small number of classic pieces from the past. I am not advocating the widespread teaching of the history of economic thought. Much of what was written in the past has been overtaken: economics has made progress. But some contributions by the great economists remain almost timeless in their continued relevance.

I set out four articles written in the third quarter of the twentieth century, each of which seems to me to provide powerful insights into how the highly connected economy of the 21st century operates.

I suggest a book on economic history which focuses on the period around 1900, when giant companies first began to appear and the foundations of global capitalism were laid down.

There is a reference to Keynes's *magnum opus*. Much of his work has been completely simplified and distorted. He was an exceptionally subtle economist who understood the importance of networks, psychology, and the limits to knowledge. The reader is guided to those chapters where these themes are set out.

Finally, there are four references on networks. Two of these are meant for the general reader.

The third is a highly technical piece from 15 years ago, which was the first really modern extension of Schelling's 'binary choice with externalities' model. It gives a flavour of what has since become a very large and highly mathematical literature on containment and diffusion in networks.

The final one is again based on modern research methodologies in this area. It describes a large computer-based tournament of competitive strategies in an evolutionary environment. It shows the advantage of a simple copying strategy. Although it is densely written, it is mainly in English.

Nobel Prize lectures

Akerlof, G. A. (2001) Behavioral macroeconomics and macroeconomic behavior (https://www.nobelprize.org/nobel_prizes/economic-sciences/laureates/2001/akerlof-lecture.pdf).

Hayek, F. A. (1974) The pretence of knowledge (https://www.nobelprize.org/nobel_prizes/economic-sciences/laureates/1974/hayek-lecture.html).

Kahneman, D. (2002) Maps of bounded rationality: a perspective on intuitive judgment and choice (https://www.nobelprize.org/nobel_prizes/economic-sciences/laureates/2002/kahnemann-lecture.pdf).

Ostrom, E. (2009) Beyond markets and states: polycentric governance of complex economic systems (https://www.nobelprize.org/nobel_prizes/economic-sciences/laureates/2009/ostrom_lecture.pdf).

Shiller, R. (2013) Speculative asset prices (https://www.nobelprize.org/nobel_prizes/economic-sciences/laureates/2013/shiller-lecture.pdf).

Smith, V. (2002) Constructivist and ecological rationality in economics (https://www.nobelprize.org/nobel_prizes/economic-sciences/laureates/2002/smith-lecture.pdf).

Stiglitz, J. E. (2001) Information and the change in the paradigm in economics (https://www.nobelprize.org/nobel_prizes/economic-sciences/laureates/2001/stiglitz-lecture.pdf).

Four classic papers

Alchian, A. A. (1950) Uncertainty, evolution, and economic theory. *Journal of Political Economy* 58(3): 211–21.

Akerlof, G. A. (1970) The market for 'lemons': quality uncertainty and the market mechanism. *Quarterly Journal of Economics* 84(3): 488–500.

Schelling, T. C. (1973) Hockey helmets, concealed weapons, and daylight saving: a study of binary choices with externalities. *Journal of Conflict Resolution* 17(3): 381–428.

Simon, H. A. (1955) A behavioral model of rational choice. *Quarterly Journal of Economics* 69(1): 99–118.

Some economic history: when the world became global

Chandler, A. (1990) *Scale and Scope: The Dynamics of Industrial Capitalism.* Harvard University Press.

Keynes and psychology

Keynes, J. M. (1936) *The General Theory of Employment, Interest and Money*, Chapters 5, 12 and 22 (many editions).

Networks and their behavioural implications

Ormerod, P. (2012) *Positive Linking: How Networks and Incentives Can Revolutionise the World.* London: Faber and Faber.

Watts, D. (2011) *Everything Is Obvious: Once You Know the Answer.* New York: Crown Business.

Watts, D. (2002) A simple model of global cascades on random networks. *Proceedings of the National Academy of Sciences* 99(9): 5766–71.

Rendell, L., Boyd, R. and many others (2010) Why copy others? Insights from the social learning tournament. *Science*, 9 April.

ABOUT THE IEA

The Institute is a research and educational charity (No. CC 235 351), limited by guarantee. Its mission is to improve understanding of the fundamental institutions of a free society by analysing and expounding the role of markets in solving economic and social problems.

The IEA achieves its mission by:

- a high-quality publishing programme
- conferences, seminars, lectures and other events
- outreach to school and college students
- brokering media introductions and appearances

The IEA, which was established in 1955 by the late Sir Antony Fisher, is an educational charity, not a political organisation. It is independent of any political party or group and does not carry on activities intended to affect support for any political party or candidate in any election or referendum, or at any other time. It is financed by sales of publications, conference fees and voluntary donations.

In addition to its main series of publications, the IEA also publishes (jointly with the University of Buckingham), *Economic Affairs*.

The IEA is aided in its work by a distinguished international Academic Advisory Council and an eminent panel of Honorary Fellows. Together with other academics, they review prospective IEA publications, their comments being passed on anonymously to authors. All IEA papers are therefore subject to the same rigorous independent refereeing process as used by leading academic journals.

IEA publications enjoy widespread classroom use and course adoptions in schools and universities. They are also sold throughout the world and often translated/reprinted.

Since 1974 the IEA has helped to create a worldwide network of 100 similar institutions in over 70 countries. They are all independent but share the IEA's mission.

Views expressed in the IEA's publications are those of the authors, not those of the Institute (which has no corporate view), its Managing Trustees, Academic Advisory Council members or senior staff.

Members of the Institute's Academic Advisory Council, Honorary Fellows, Trustees and Staff are listed on the following page.

The Institute gratefully acknowledges financial support for its publications programme and other work from a generous benefaction by the late Professor Ronald Coase.

The Institute of Economic Affairs
2 Lord North Street, Westminster, London SW1P 3LB
Tel: 020 7799 8900
Fax: 020 7799 2137
Email: iea@iea.org.uk
Institute of
Economic Affairs   Internet: iea.org.uk

Other books recently published by the IEA include:

Advertising in a Free Society
Ralph Harris and Arthur Seldon
With an introduction by Christopher Snowdon
Hobart Paper 176; ISBN 978-0-255-36696-0; £12.50

Selfishness, Greed and Capitalism: Debunking Myths about the Free Market
Christopher Snowdon
Hobart Paper 177; ISBN 978-0-255-36677-9; £12.50

Waging the War of Ideas
John Blundell
Occasional Paper 131; ISBN 978-0-255-36684-7; £12.50

Brexit: Directions for Britain Outside the EU
Ralph Buckle, Tim Hewish, John C. Hulsman, Iain Mansfield and
Robert Oulds
Hobart Paperback 178; ISBN 978-0-255-36681-6; £12.50

Flaws and Ceilings – Price Controls and the Damage They Cause
Edited by Christopher Coyne and Rachel Coyne
Hobart Paperback 179; ISBN 978-0-255-36701-1; £12.50

*Scandinavian Unexceptionalism: Culture, Markets and the Failure of
Third-Way Socialism*
Nima Sanandaji
Readings in Political Economy 1; ISBN 978-0-255-36704-2; £10.00

Classical Liberalism – A Primer
Eamonn Butler
Readings in Political Economy 2; ISBN 978-0-255-36707-3; £10.00

Federal Britain: The Case for Decentralisation
Philip Booth
Readings in Political Economy 3; ISBN 978-0-255-36713-4; £10.00

Forever Contemporary: The Economics of Ronald Coase
Edited by Cento Veljanovski
Readings in Political Economy 4; ISBN 978-0-255-36710-3; £15.00

Power Cut? How the EU Is Pulling the Plug on Electricity Markets
Carlo Stagnaro
Hobart Paperback 180; ISBN 978-0-255-36716-5; £10.00

Policy Stability and Economic Growth – Lessons from the Great Recession
John B. Taylor
Readings in Political Economy 5; ISBN 978-0-255-36719-6; £7.50

Breaking Up Is Hard To Do: Britain and Europe's Dysfunctional Relationship
Edited by Patrick Minford and J. R. Shackleton
Hobart Paperback 181; ISBN 978-0-255-36722-6; £15.00

In Focus: The Case for Privatising the BBC
Edited by Philip Booth
Hobart Paperback 182; ISBN 978-0-255-36725-7; £12.50

Islamic Foundations of a Free Society
Edited by Nouh El Harmouzi and Linda Whetstone
Hobart Paperback 183; ISBN 978-0-255-36728-8; £12.50

The Economics of International Development: Foreign Aid versus Freedom for the World's Poor
William Easterly
Readings in Political Economy 6; ISBN 978–0–255–36731–8; £7.50

Taxation, Government Spending and Economic Growth
Edited by Philip Booth
Hobart Paperback 184; ISBN 978–0–255–36734–9; £15.00

Universal Healthcare without the NHS: Towards a Patient-Centred Health System
Kristian Niemietz
Hobart Paperback 185; ISBN 978–0–255–36737–0; £10.00

Sea Change: How Markets and Property Rights Could Transform the Fishing Industry
Edited by Richard Wellings
Readings in Political Economy 7; ISBN 978–0–255–36740–0; £10.00

Working to Rule: The Damaging Economics of UK Employment Regulation
J. R. Shackleton
Hobart Paperback 186; ISBN 978-0-255-36743-1; £15.00

Education, War and Peace: The Surprising Success of Private Schools in War-Torn Countries
James Tooley and David Longfield
ISBN 978-0-255-36746-2; £10.00

Killjoys: A Critique of Paternalism
Christopher Snowdon
ISBN 978-0-255-36749-3; £12.50

Financial Stability without Central Banks
George Selgin, Kevin Dowd and Mathieu Bédard
ISBN 978-0-255-36752-3; £10.00

Other IEA publications

Comprehensive information on other publications and the wider work of the IEA can be found at www.iea.org.uk. To order any publication please see below.

Personal customers

Orders from personal customers should be directed to the IEA:

Clare Rusbridge
IEA
2 Lord North Street
FREEPOST LON10168
London SW1P 3YZ
Tel: 020 7799 8907. Fax: 020 7799 2137
Email: sales@iea.org.uk

Trade customers

All orders from the book trade should be directed to the IEA's distributor:

NBN International (IEA Orders)
Orders Dept.
NBN International
10 Thornbury Road
Plymouth PL6 7PP
Tel: 01752 202301, Fax: 01752 202333
Email: orders@nbninternational.com

IEA subscriptions

The IEA also offers a subscription service to its publications. For a single annual payment (currently £42.00 in the UK), subscribers receive every monograph the IEA publishes. For more information please contact:

Clare Rusbridge
Subscriptions
IEA
2 Lord North Street
FREEPOST LON10168
London SW1P 3YZ
Tel: 020 7799 8907, Fax: 020 7799 2137
Email: crusbridge@iea.org.uk